ABOUT THE AUTHOR

Daniel Pambianchi is the founder and CEO of Cadenza Wines Inc. and GM of Maleta Winery in Niagara-on-the-Lake, Ontario; Technical Editor for *WineMaker* magazine; a member of the American Wine Society and the Society of Wine Educators; and author of *Techniques in Home Winemaking: The Comprehensive Guide to Making Château-Style Wines.*

Contents

Preface

Congratulations!

You have decided to start making your own wine at home ... from a kit—basically concentrate or a blend of concentrate and grape juice packaged in a box with all the necessary additives to make wine. Whether it is out of pleasure of crafting your own wine or to consistently replicate your favorite style and at a low cost, making wine at home is easy. And your wine will definitely impress your friends and family, many who will not believe that the wine is from a kit; indeed, the quality of wine kits has improved in leaps and bounds over the last decade. Wine judges at amateur competitions are repeatedly impressed by the increasing quality of homemade kit wines, often indistinguishable from their fresh juice or grape counterparts.

If you ever doubted the ability to make great wine from kits while investing little time and equipment, there is no better time to jump on the kit-winemaking bandwagon. Statistical data show that not only is wine consumption on the rise, increasing at a faster pace than other alcoholic drinks, but also that the number of home winemakers is ever increasing. And with the plethora of wine kits and styles now available, all indications are that this has become a very serious hobby.

If you have never made wine and are not familiar with what is involved but you want to start slow and easy, this book is for you—it is for the true beginner. It is intended to supplement the instructions provided with kits. Detailed, step-by-step instructions and illustrations will lead you through the process of making great wines at home and answer questions that may come up but which are not addressed in the manufacturers' instruction sheet. And if you run into problems, rest assured, we will also help you fix those.

Specifically:

Chapter 1 provides an overview of winemaking concepts and an introduction to the important terminology, and why you should make wine from a kit.

Chapter 2 describes the different kinds of wine kits to shed light on the differences in quality between, for example, a four- and an eight-week kit. It also provides an overview of what you will find in a kit and what kind of wine styles you can expect to make from it.

Chapter 3 lists and explains the use of all the necessary equipment you need to make your first batch of wine from a kit.

Chapter 4 provides day-by-day, step-by-step instructions on making your first batch of wine from a kit.

Chapter 5 lists common problems often encountered by new and sometimes also seasoned winemakers, and gives instructions on how to avoid or correct such problems.

Chapter 6 discusses important advanced topics, such as sulfite management, cold stabilization and blending, to help you transition to the next level of winemaking.

A handy glossary is available at the back of this book to help you become a knowledgeable winemaker.

When you do make the leap to bigger winemaking projects, particularly if you decide to tackle winemaking from grapes, please refer to my other publication, *Techniques in Home Winemaking: The Comprehensive Guide to Making Château-Style Wines* (Montréal: Véhicule Press, 2008).

Daniel Pambianchi, April 2009

Acknowledgments

No matter how simple a book project may seem, it always involves a great deal of support from many people. This book is no exception, and I am indebted to Simon Dardick and Nancy Marrelli, publishers of Véhicule Press, and their team, Irving Dardick (Pathology Images Inc.) for "piecing" together my work in his usual professional ways, and Don Martin for a wonderful job on the illustrations. As well, I would like to thank the many reviewers who have provided comments and feedback on the manuscript; specifically, Sigrid Gertsen-Briand of Lallemand North America, Dr. Matteo Meglioli of Mosti Mondiale Inc., Dr. Eric L. Gibbs of High-Q, Inc., and Chris Opela of Brewmaster Inc.

1

Introduction

Kit wines are no longer the dreaded poor man's wines of yesteryear. Production technologies and processes, coupled with fruit sourced from top-rated vineyards around the world, have greatly improved the juice and therefore the wine quality of kits. Many well-made kit wines can now rival those made from grapes—in some cases, even commercial wines—and the proof is in competition results. Wines are often indistinguishable, with kit wines scoring higher with judges in blind tastings.

WHY MAKE WINE FROM A KIT?

Making wine from kits is easy and relatively cheap compared with making wine from grapes; and with the proliferation of brew-on-premise and bulk wine operations, "making" or bottling your own could not be easier. Many people get into winemaking mainly for the pleasure of making their own, from start to finish.

For beginners, wine kits are ideal since the risk of failure is minimized because all ingredients are prepackaged in premeasured quantities and the concentrate is balanced and ready for making wine. Kits require little or no "correction," or adjustment, for sugar, alcohol and acidity—the kit manufacturer has taken care of all that balancing. Reconstituted grape juice may also be sold separately without the necessary additives; but these are recommended for more experienced winemakers only because additives need to be selected separately and measured accurately.

Making wine from grapes requires a more significant investment in equipment, it is messier and requires considerably more work and effort, and can be quite risky, even in the hands of a proficient winemaker who must deal with the oft-unbalanced chemistry in grapes and juice; however, the biggest drawback is sourcing good fruit to make consistently good wine year after year. Wine can vary significantly in quality, perhaps even style, from year to year even when the fruit is sourced from the same vineyard. And this is exactly the major attraction of kit winemaking—consistency. The same quality and style of wine can be repeated every time and any time of the year, whenever you want. With kits providing all the necessary additives to make just about any kind or style of wine, it doesn't get any easier.

WINEMAKING 101

So how is wine from a kit actually made?

We first introduce a high-level review of the winemaking process and lingo; important terms that you should become familiar with are identified in italics and are also listed in a glossary at the back of this book. As well, names of yeast species (e.g., *S. cerevisiae*), which are typically derived from Greek or Latin names, are always italicized.

Here, the term *concentrate* is used for referring to concentrated juice or a blend of concentrated juice and grape juice, unless a distinction is necessary.

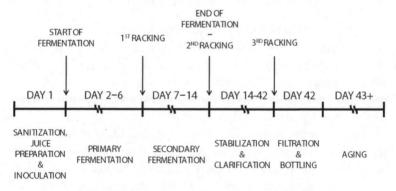

Figure 1.1. Typical six-week kit winemaking timeline

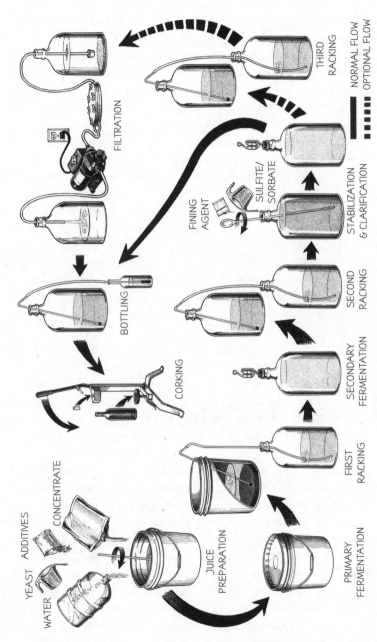

Figure 1.2. Kit winemaking process flowchart

Winemaking refers to the process for producing wine, from juice preparation to bottling, by fermenting juice from grapes or other fruits. Unfermented juice, the starting raw material, is called *must*; once it starts fermenting and alcohol is being produced, it is called *wine*.

The major process steps in winemaking include: (1) sanitization, (2) juice preparation, (3) fermentation, (4) stabilization and clarification, (5) filtration, and (6) bottling and aging. Fig. 1.1 shows a typical winemaking timeline for a six-week kit with the process steps mapped. Fig. 1.2 illustrates a generalized process flowchart.

Sanitization refers to the process of washing and sanitizing all equipment, before any winemaking, to eliminate or inhibit microbes and avoid the risk of microbial contamination of the juice or wine, which could otherwise cause irreversible spoilage.

In kit winemaking, *juice preparation* simply involves reconstituting the concentrate by adding water, if required, to bring it to the required volume, and allowing the must (juice) to warm up or cool down to within the recommended range in preparation for fermentation. The must is then pitched, or inoculated, with yeast—a process known as *inoculation*— to enable fermentation. The strains of yeast used in winemaking belong to the species *Saccharomyces cerevisiae* (*S. cerevisiae*) or *Saccharomyces bayanus* (*S. bayanus*).

NOTE: A new yeast taxonomy proposes that all wine yeast strains belong to the pecies *S. cerevisiae*, further qualified by the race—either *cerevisiae* or *bayanus*; hence, you may see wine yeasts referenced in literature as either *S. cerevisiae* race *cerevisiae* or as *S. cerevisiae* race *bayanus*.

S. cerevisiae strains are the most common because these are well suited for a wide range of winemaking applications. *S. bayanus* strains are most often used under difficult fermentation conditions or to restart a stuck or sluggish fermentation. Given the fermentation power of *S. bayanus* yeast, kits are almost always supplied with strains of this yeast.

Fermentation, or more precisely, *yeast* or *alcoholic fermentation* in winemaking, is the chemical process of converting sugar in must into alcohol under the action of yeast with carbon dioxide (CO_2) gas as a by-product. The amount of alcohol (ethanol) produced is directly proportional to the amount of sugar present in the must and which is fermented. Any unfermented sugar, called *residual sugar (RS)*, will result in a sweeter wine. It follows then that alcohol content can be increased by adding sugar, a practice known as *chaptalization*, which is also used for making sweet wines—that is, by adding sugar at the end of fermentation.

A *dry* wine has almost no residual sugar and no perceptible sweetness. As the amount of residual sugar and perceptible sweetness increases, wines are termed *off-dry, medium-dry, medium-sweet* and *sweet.* For example, premium Cabernet Sauvignon, Pinot Noir, or oaked Chardonnay will (should) be dry, a White Zinfandel will be medium-dry to medium-sweet, and port- or ice wine-style wines will be sweet.

Although wine undergoes a single alcoholic fermentation, it is common in home winemaking to refer to "primary" and "secondary fermentations" to describe arbitrary phases relative to the amount of sugar still present in the wine; it is usually related to fermentation vigor. The transition from the vigorous *primary fermentation* to the lesser active *secondary fermentation* signals the need to transfer the wine to another container to protect it from spoilage. This procedure of transferring wine from one container to another, while leaving behind sediment formed in the first container, is called *racking.*

> NOTE: The above terminology can be confusing as *secondary fermentation* is used for referring to a non-alcoholic fermentation (that occurs in wines made from fresh juice or grapes), known as *malolactic fermentation,* which usually follows the alcoholic fermentation. Refer to section on malolactic fermentation in Chapter 6 for more information.

Sediment resulting from yeast activity during alcoholic fermentation is called *lees.* When wine is racked from its lees from one container to another, there is some loss of wine because of the volume taken up by sediment. The resulting headspace, or *ullage,* in the receiving container must be replaced, or *topped up,* with wine or water to minimize wine exposure to air. Air is wine's worst enemy. Wine affected by excessive exposure to air is said to be *oxidized.*

Stabilization is the process of readying the wine for consumption or aging to ensure that clarity, freshness and balance of the wine are maintained. Stabilization also protects the wine from microbial spoilage, refermentation and premature oxidation while the wine is aging and once in bottle. Stabilization is a necessary step before bottling or bulk aging of wine for an extended period of time. The most common stabilizing agents used in home winemaking include: *potassium metabisulfite*—commonly referred to simply as *sulfite* and often abbreviated to *KMS*—used as an antioxidant, antibacterial and preservative; and *potassium sorbate*, used for preventing renewed fermentation in bottled wine. *Sulfur dioxide (SO_2)*, a component of sulfite, is the actual compound that provides protection although the term is often used interchangeably with *sulfite*. Sulfite is available as a powder or 0.44-g *Campden tablets*, and is used for preparing a sulfite solution for sanitizing equipment or for adding to wine. Campden tablets must first be crushed before being dissolved in water.

Clarification is the process of removing particles still in suspension in wine and which affect clarity and limpidity. Clarification can be achieved by *fining* using additives, commonly known as *clarifying* or *fining agents*, by mechanical filtration, or both. Fining agents are added to wine to coagulate particles in suspension and cause them to sediment. A subsequent racking is required when fining, to separate particles and lees that have sedimented. *Filtration* is the process of passing wine through a filter medium by mechanical means to separate particles in suspension.

Before bottling, different batches of wine are often blended to achieve a desired style or to improve balance in color, taste, smell and mouthfeel, or what are collectively known as the *organoleptic qualities*. The final blend will exhibit the desired organoleptic qualities inherited from the various blending wines. Kits are designed to produce specific styles of wine by *blending* different kinds of juice during the kit manufacturing process, and so, there is no blending of wines required during winemaking.

Bottling is the final winemaking operation where wine is transferred from bulk containers to bottles for further aging or for drinking. Bottled wine must be properly sealed with appropriate closures, such as corks, to protect it from the elements.

Bottle or bulk *aging* refers to the *maturation* or *cellaring* phase of winemaking, necessary for wine to develop its character, structure and complexity. The aging period can vary from a few months to several years depending on the quality of juice used and wine produced as well as winemaking techniques.

CONTAINS SULFITES

Consumers have become more aware of the presence and the role of sulfite in wines owing to the mandatory mention *Contains Sulfites* on all wine sold in the U.S., and to an increasing concern of additives in food and beverages. And many blame sulfites as the cause of headaches after drinking wine, particularly red wine.

Recent research has shed some light on this controversy as only a very small segment of the population—approximately 1%—is allergic, exhibiting asthmatic reactions, not headaches. In fact, very few people, if any, actually complain of headaches after drinking white wines, which typically contain higher levels of sulfite as these are more prone to spoilage effects and therefore need added protection.

So why are people getting a headache when drinking (in moderation) red wine? Histamine.

Histamine is a biogenic amine that is believed to cause headaches with some doctors recommending taking antihistamine tablets before drinking red wine if one is susceptible.

Where does it come from? Histamine is a by-product of malolactic fermentation (see the section on malolactic fermentation in Chapter 6)—a technique mainly used in red winemaking—where lactic acid bacteria convert malic acid into lactic acid. Only some types of bacteria produce histamine, and therefore, only those red wines processed with histamine-producing bacteria will contain histamine. How can we, the consumers, tell? We can't.

And are there sulfite-free wines? No. Sulfite, or more specifically, sulfur dioxide (SO_2), is a natural by-product of fermentation, albeit in small quantities, and therefore, wine can never be totally free of sulfite.

2

Winemaking Kits

Today, four-, five-, six- and eight-week kits for making 23 L (6 gal) or 30 standard 750-mL bottles of wine from concentrate or a blend of concentrate and grape juice are very popular among wine hobbyists, especially beginners. Kits are now available in a wide array of styles for every palate; whether you like a light-bodied Sauvignon Blanc, a fruity Burgundian-style, oaked Chardonnay, or a full-bodied Cabernet Sauvignon–Shiraz blend, there is a kit for you.

> NOTE: Kits that make 23 L (6 gal) of wine are now the most popular and readily available on the market, although you may still find those that yield 20 L (5 gal). In this book, we use the 23-L (6-gal) format to describe the process and rates of additions of ingredients.

Concentrate in kits is processed by manufacturers to remove some water, and is pasteurized to eradicate wild yeasts and other unwanted spoilage organisms; sulfite is added to make it stable and to extend its shelf life. The concentrate, which can contain varietal juice, can be a single varietal or a blend of two or more varietals to allow the kit to produce the style of wine desired.

What differentiates one kit from another is the quality of the raw material—that is, the grapes or juice used for making the concentrate—the concentration process, and style of wine. As a general rule, the lower the concentration, the better the quality of the concentrate and, therefore, the finished wine; but it will also command a higher price. Why is that?

Lower concentration means more concentrate volume, and in winemaking, the concentrate is said to have a lower Brix, which is a measure of the density of sugar (more on Brix later). And lower-Brix kits typically contain better quality raw material and from premium sources, and suffer the least from the effects of pasteurization, namely the high heat to process the raw material. Higher-Brix kits—that is, those packaged in smaller volumes—will suffer most from pasteurization where the required higher heat and slower processing will tend to cause a browning reaction from sugars, amino acids and proteins, and to increase volatility (loss) of aromatic compounds in aromas and flavors. The higher Brix will also impede the tannin balance process because tannins, when needed to be added, are less soluble in less water. This is particularly true of red concentrates, which have a much higher concentration of tannins.

The following sections describe the different kinds of wine kits and styles of wines.

KINDS OF WINE KITS

Wine kits consist of concentrate packaged in polyethylene bags in a variety of volumes, and come complete with simple instructions for problem-free winemaking. The kits include various "ingredients" or additives to enable the winemaking process and to achieve the desired style of wine.

There are four main kinds of kits available, in increasing order of quality of the raw material and the finished wine: concentrate-only, concentrate and fresh juice, premium, and ultra-premium.

Concentrate-only kits

Concentrate-only raw material is used in four-week kits for making light, early drinking wines; these kits are typically the least expensive. The concentrate has the highest Brix of all the kinds of raw material; therefore, wine from four-week kits is meant for quick fermentation, processing and bottling, and is meant to be drunk young—that is, soon after bottling. The small volume of concentrate, typically between 7.5 and 10 L

(2 and 2½ gal), is reconstituted by adding water up to the 23-L (6-gal) level, as per the kits' instructions.

Concentrate and fresh juice kits
Five- and six-week wine kits containing a blend of concentrate and fresh juice as the raw material are also available for making wine with more body than their concentrate-only counterparts. The wines can be enjoyed in just a few weeks, and will undoubtedly improve with a few months of cellaring. The addition of fresh juice decreases Brix, meaning that these are packaged in bigger volumes, typically 10 or 12 L (2½ or 3 gal).

Premium kits
Premium, six-week kits consist of concentrate plus varietal grape juice, and are larger in volume, for example, 16 L (4 gal), and so require less water to reconstitute the juice to the 23-L level, or up to 23 L (6 gal) that do not require any water to be added. They have a lower Brix than their concentrate-only and concentrate-and-fresh-juice counterparts. Some kits also come with dried grape skins to add more body, color and mouthfeel. Premium kit wines have better aging potential and should be cellared for a few months to a year before drinking to allow the amalgam of aromas, flavors and taste to integrate and develop to their peak potential.

Owing to the varietal grape juice added to the concentrate, wines from premium kits are much more typical of the intended style and tend to be fuller-bodied.

Ultra-premium kits
Ultra-premium, eight-week kits are similar to premium, six-week kits but contain a higher ratio of varietal grape juice sourced from specific, premium grape-growing regions, often down to single vineyards, and so are most expressive of that region's style. Red wine kits can also contain "fresh" or dried grape skins to add more body, color and mouthfeel.

Ultra-premium kits are packaged in volumes of 18 L (4½ gal) and have the lowest Brix of all raw materials found in kits; therefore, the wines are fuller-bodied with the longest aging potential. Wines must be cellared for at least one year to eighteen months to allow the wine to develop to its intended style and to express its full potential. Wines made from these kits can surpass the quality of wines made from fresh juice and even grapes, and often rival the quality of some commercial wines.

NOTE: Some kits specify the weight in lb or kg instead of volume of concentrate. Weight and volume are directly proportional with 1 L of concentrate weighing, on average, approximately 1.1 kg (2½ lb).

WHAT IS INCLUDED IN A WINE KIT

A kit, as the name implies, includes everything you need (see Fig. 2.1) to make a batch of wine for the desired style. Specifically, you will find: concentrate, yeast, clarifying agents, sulfite, potassium sorbate and other additives, such as oak chips, depending on wine style; some also include ready-to-apply labels.

The concentrate comes packaged in a polyethylene bag in one of the various volumes depending on the kind of kit. Most require the addition of water, but some styles, for example, concentrate for ice wine-style wine, do not, and so follow instructions.

Most kits include a strong yeast type that performs well under variable and often less-than-ideal conditions to reduce the risk of fermentation problems. Some kits also include a package of yeast nutrients, or DAP (diammonium phosphate), to boost the yeast's fermentation ability, reducing the risk of a stuck or sluggish fermentation. Yeast nutrients may have already been added to the concentrate by the manufacturer.

One or more clarifying or fining agents are used for clarifying the

Figure 2.1. Typical components of a six-week wine kit

wine before final filtration and bottling to get a crystal clear wine. Bentonite and kieselsol paired with gelatin or chitosan (a shellfish derivative) are the most common clarifying agents included with kits. Bentonite is a natural absorptive type of clay that binds to and precipitates suspended particles. Kieselsol is a silicate suspension that electrostatically binds and precipitates proteins.

Kieselsol, and gelatin or chitosan come in two separate packages—they are added at different times at the end of fermentation.

Isinglass, a pure gelatin prepared from the swim bladders of cichlids (tropical spiny-finned freshwater fish), is also used because it acts quickly and it strips color to a lesser extent than other protein-based fining agents such as gelatin.

Sulfite, or more specifically potassium metabisulfite (KMS), is a preservative commonly used in the food and beverage industry. It is essential to protect wine from oxidation and potential spoilage microbes.

Potassium sorbate is a common food and beverage additive used for inhibiting growth of yeast and mold. In winemaking, its main application is in stabilizing wines with residual sugar to prevent renewed yeast activity and fermentation once the wine is bottled. Any residual sugar can potentially restart fermentation if there is any yeast. If wine starts refermenting, it can cause bottles to explode. Note that potassium sorbate cannot be used for stopping an active fermentation; it can only inhibit a renewed fermentation.

Depending on the kind and style of wine you are making, the kit may include other additives such as oak chips, tannins and dried elderberries. These are intended to be used as instructed to achieve the desired style, for example, to add oak aromas and flavor complexities, and mouthfeel and body. Following is a list of other additives you may find in a kit and their purpose.

Grape by-products

Fresh or dried grape skins are used for increasing color, body and mouthfeel for fuller-bodied reds—there are no grape by-products in white wine kits. Fresh or dried grape skins are added directly to the must at the juice preparation stage.

Oak

Oak powder, shavings and chips are used in premium reds and select whites, such as Chardonnay, to impart oak aromas and flavors for added character and complexity. Toasted oak can additionally impart aromas of vanilla, caramel, coffee, chocolate and aromatic sweetness.

Tannins

Tannins, in the form of powder, are added to red wine to improve body, structure and mouthfeel by increasing astringency. Tannins may already have been added to the concentrate by the manufacturer. Tannins are not added to white wines although some concentrate may contain a small amount to hasten clarification when the kit uses gelatin.

Enzymes

Pectic enzymes improve fining and filtering operations of high-pectin white and red wines by breaking down pectin, which occur naturally in wine but are often the cause of cloudiness. Some manufacturers may already have added pectic enzymes to their concentrate. You will find pectic enzymes packaged with fruit wine kits, because fruits have much higher pectin contents than grape juice.

Elderberries or other dried fruits or flowers

Some kits use dried fruits or flowers, or both, to impart specific aromas and flavors to wine to replicate the desired wine style. For example, elderberries are used for adding spicy or peppery notes to red wines.

Glycerin

Glycerin, or glycerol, is used for increasing mouthfeel and body or perceived sweetness.

Sugar

Kits meant to produce a sweeter-style wine will contain some form of sugar, for example, liquid-invert sugar, also called a *conditioner*, or a blend of liquid-invert sugar and grape juice concentrate. Sugar-containing additives also contain sulfite and sorbate to ensure that these remain stable while in the kits' package or that sweetened wines will not start refermenting.

Metatartaric acid

Metatartaric acid is an ingredient added to wine just before bottling to prevent tartrate deposits—harmless, colorless crystals, also known as *wine diamonds*—which are the result of wine being subjected to cold temperatures. You can expect this in premium and ultra-premium wines but not in the four- or five-week kits, which have already been tartrate-stabilized during the production process; more on this in Chapter 6.

WINE STYLES

Many different styles of wine are now available which are otherwise not available as grape juice or grapes, such as Bordeaux, Chablis, port and ice wine (Icewine). With international wine production regulations now restricting the labeling of musts and wines to reflect their true appellation of origin, home winemakers need to inquire or confirm the contents of the concentrate. For example, concentrates from California or other parts of the world can no longer be labeled "Bordeaux" unless they are truly from that region. Alternatively, different styles can be created with additives supplied with kits.

There are now a whole host of kits for making many different styles of wine from fruit sourced from all the major grape-growing regions of the world. You can now make port-, sherry- and ice wine-style wines as well as sparkling wine from kits. The following is an overview of some of the more common styles.

A dry wine is a style of wine with no perceptible sweetness. Almost all red wines are dry, with a few exceptions, like port-style wine, because sweetness in reds would throw off the delicate balance between mouthfeel and acidity. Whites come in a range of increasing sweetness from dry to off-dry, medium-dry, medium-sweet, or sweet. An off-dry white has just a hint of perceptible sweetness, but this is often difficult to detect when the acidity is high.

Varietals are wines made from single grape varieties whose style is most characteristic and representative of those varieties—for example, a Cabernet Sauvignon should be full-bodied with a richly concentrated red color and with oak notes and peppery aromas; whereas a Riesling should be light and refreshing, perhaps dry, off-dry, or maybe even medium-sweet. The most common and most popular varietals in reds include Cabernet Sauvignon, Merlot and Pinot Noir, while Chardonnay, Sauvignon Blanc and Riesling are popular varietals in whites.

Bordeaux-style refers to a blend of red varietals, usually Cabernet Sauvignon, Cabernet Franc and Merlot, which mimics wines from the famed winemaking region of France; the wines will tend to be medium- to full-bodied with some oak character.

Burgundian-style, in reds, refers to a Pinot Noir varietal and, in whites, to a Chardonnay varietal. These are excellent wines that can range from simple and light to complex and full-bodied, and are meant to mimic those styles produced in Burgundy, France. Chablis-style refers to a Chardonnay varietal that mimics the fuller-bodied style from the more specific region of Chablis in Burgundy.

Rosé, also known as *blush*, is a pink-colored wine made from red grape varieties using white winemaking techniques (although it can be made from a blend of white and red wines) and can range from dry to medium-sweet in style. *White Zinfandel* is a term commonly used in the U.S. for a sweeter-style blush wine.

Port-style wine is a fortified, sweet red wine with an alcohol level typically around 20% and which replicates port wine made in the Oporto region in Portugal's Douro Valley. In true port production, no sugar is added; instead, while the wine is still fermenting, a distilled spirit, such as brandy, is added to stop the fermentation—the sudden addition and high alcohol of brandy will inhibit any yeast activity—and the wine retains natural sugar and high alcohol. The wine is then aged in oak barrels to add further aroma and flavor complexities. There are many port wine styles depending on maturation (aging) and methods for imparting oak aromas and flavors, and include ruby, tawny, vintage and late-bottled vintage (LBV) ports.

Sherry-style is a fortified white wine that can range from dry to sweet, depending on style, and replicates sherry wine made in Spain's Jerez region. Similar to port production, brandy is added to fortify wine; however, the wine is left to ferment to dryness before fortification. Fino sherry is the driest and, using various winemaking techniques, different styles and levels of sweetness can be created, such as manzanilla, amontillado, oloroso and cream sherry.

Ice wine-style is a very sweet wine that mimics the style of those luscious wines from Ontario and British Columbia, Canada as well as Germany. True ice wine can only be made from harvested grapes that have frozen naturally on vines. Since the water content in grape berries is frozen, only the sweet syrup is extracted and fermented. The result is a delectable, sweet wine with peach, apricot and litchi aromas and flavors. The most popular varietals in whites are Vidal and Riesling, although kits are usually blends of other white varietals, and Cabernet Franc in reds, although, again, kits are generally blends of other varietals.

Sparkling wine, or *bubbly*, is a wine with carbon dioxide (CO_2) produced by enabling a second alcoholic fermentation through the addition of sugar and yeast, as opposed to injecting CO_2 as in soft-drink production. *Méthode traditionelle* (traditional method) sparkling wines, such as champagne, are produced by carrying out the second fermentation in the bottle to trap the gas and aging on the lees in the bottle. *Cuve close* or Charmat-method sparkling wines are produced by carrying out the second fermentation in bulk in tanks, which significantly cuts down on production costs. Sparkling wines are usually white, often rosé, and now, we are starting to see some red bubbly wines too.

Some manufacturers now provide an easy-to-understand, triple 0-to-5 scale for levels of oak, body and sweetness of the finished wine so you know exactly what to expect. For example, a full-bodied, oaked Chardonnay might be represented by 3–4–0 as you would expect it to be dry, whereas Gewürztraminer might be represented as 0–3–2 since it is often off-dry or lightly sweet but not oaked. You can expect many reds to have some level of oak (2–4) with usually high body (3–5) and almost always dry (0).

BEHIND THE SCENES IN KIT PRODUCTION

Wine kit production technology has progressed significantly over the last decade, which has improved the quality of concentrates on the market and the resulting wine. Here is a look at the technology and processes used for creating concentrate for making wine.

Kit manufacturers source grapes from vineyards around the world from both northern and southern hemispheres to have a constant supply throughout the year. Concentrates are (must be) produced year-round, unlike winemaking in each specific region, which happens only once a year.

But as growers and wineries, kit manufacturers too harvest grapes based not only on "the numbers"—Brix/SG, total acidity, and pH—but also on physiological and sensorial (organoleptic) characteristics, such as color and flavors, which must be balanced with the chemistry of the grapes.

Once harvested, white varietal grapes are crushed and pressed, and the juice is transferred to tanks to allow unwanted solids to settle. The juice is stabilized with sulfite, and then enzymes that break down pectin, and bentonite are added, both of which play a critical role in clarifying the juice as well as, ultimately, the wine. The juice is further stabilized at very cold temperatures where it is then separated from the heavy deposit at the bottom of the tank, and filtered. The juice must be maintained cold to prevent fermentation from starting on its own.

In the case of red varietals, where color must be extracted during the juice processing stage (as opposed to during fermentation in winemaking), grapes are crushed and allowed to macerate with the juice in a tank at cold temperatures to prevent fermentation from starting on its own. Special enzymes are added to extract color and aromas from the grape skins; this is the most critical step in producing red juice of high organoleptic quality. When the desired quality is achieved, the grapes are pressed and the juice is moved to the next stage of processing. Some grapes may be kept for shipping with kits where additional maceration is desired during winemaking.

The white or red juice is run through a concentrator to remove some of the water content and concentrate the juice. Key aromas and flavors, which may be lost during processing, are recovered and returned to the concentrate; this is the critical step that now ensures minimal loss of aromas and flavors compared with kits of yesteryear. The concentrated juice is then tartrate-stabilized by chilling to hasten precipitation of tartrates—harmless, colorless crystals—to ensure that this does not happen during winemaking or while bottles are chilled in the refrigerator.

At this point, the manufacturer decides on the quality and style of wine the kit is intended to produce. The concentrate may be blended with other concentrates to replicate, for example, a Bordeaux-style red (typically a blend of Cabernet Sauvignon, Cabernet Franc, and Merlot), or varietal juice is added for greater varietal character.

As a last step, the concentrate is pasteurized to eradicate any latent spoilage microorganisms, and is then packaged for sale.

3

Winemaking Equipment

There is minimal investment in equipment and supplies for making wine from kits. Some of the more expensive equipment, specifically those that are used only occasionally—e.g., filtration and bottling equipment—can be rented from your local home winemaking supply shop. If you will be making wine regularly or you are part of a larger group of home winemakers in your neighborhood, you may want to purchase the equipment and have it available at all times.

Following is a list of basic equipment and supplies you will need to make wine from kits. The starter fermentation equipment listed below is often sold as a starter kit for those just getting into kit winemaking.

Starter fermentation equipment (see Fig. 3.1)
• Food-grade plastic pail with lid
• 23-L (6-gal) glass carboy
• Hydrometer and test cylinder
• Floating thermometer
• Fermentation (air) lock and no. 7 bung
• Stirring spoon or paddle

- Racking cane (J-tube)
- Siphoning hose with clamp
- Gravy baster or wine thief

Supplies
- Potassium metabisulfite (KMS)

Bottling equipment (see Fig. 3.2)—most can be rented
- Filter and pump
- Bottle rinser
- Bottle drainer and sanitizer
- Filler .
- Corker

Bottling supplies (see Fig. 3.3)
- Filter pads
- Bottles
- No. 9 corks, 1½ in long
- Capsules
- Labels

Figure 3.1. Starter fermentation equipment

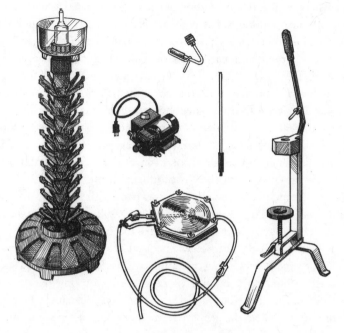

Figure 3.2. Bottling equipment

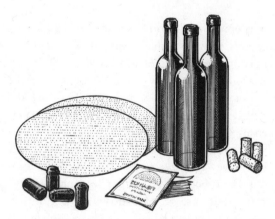

Figure 3.3. Bottling supplies

The plastic pail is used for the primary fermentation and should be a minimum of 27 L (7 gal) when used with 23-L (6-gal) kits; this is to allow for volume expansion and foaming during fermentation because there will be a great deal of carbon dioxide gas generated. Only use food-grade plastic; other kinds may contain toxic chemicals that could potentially leach into the wine. Before using the pail, accurately pour 23 L (6 gal) of water into it and mark that level with a permanent marker on the outside of the pail; pails usually do not have a graduated scale for volume (and if they do, you may want to check it the first time you use the pail). You may also want to drill a small hole in the center of the lid just big enough to seat a no. 7 bung. Some prefer to simply lay the lid loosely over the pail during fermentation while others prefer to fit the lid snugly and install a bung and fermentation lock. The choice is yours; however, the idea is to ensure that the gas produced during fermentation is allowed to escape unobstructed. The drawback with installing a fermentation lock on the lid is that the vigorous primary fermentation will cause the water or solution in the lock to splash out until it subdues.

A 23-L (6-gal) glass carboy will be used as a secondary fermenter as well as for various processing operations. Consider investing in a second carboy to minimize the number of rackings. If you only have one carboy and a pail, and need to rack three times, you will actually be racking five times; once from the primary fermenter (pail) to the secondary fermenter (carboy) in the first racking, and then twice from the carboy to the pail and back to the carboy in the second and third racking (refer to Fig. 1.2).

The hydrometer is a simple instrument to measure the concentration of sugar in the juice relative to the density of water (1.000), or *specific gravity* (*SG* or *sp gr*); or the absolute density, or *Brix* (*°B*); and provides an approximate measure of the *potential alcohol* (*PA*) of the wine if all the fermentable sugar is fermented. For example, an SG of 1.100 means the juice contains sugar that increases its density by approximately 10% relative to the density of water. Since alcohol is less dense than water and there is essentially no sugar left over in (dry) wine, the SG will be below 1.000. Note that we say *approximately* here because must contains many other dissolved solids other than sugar that influence the reading.

The most important use of the hydrometer is in monitoring fermentation progress to determine when it has completed. Be sure to **measure the SG as close as possible to the calibration temperature indicated on your hydrometer model**—most models are calibrated at 15.5°C (60°F) or 20°C (68°F), although the former is the most prevalent on the market. Some literature provides "correction tables" to compensate for readings taken at temperatures other than the calibration temperature; this is really not necessary for our purpose here because the impact on potential alcohol is trivial. You should, however, measure the SG at the end of fermentation as close to the hydrometer's calibration temperature as possible—at this point, you need to make sure that fermentation is actually complete because a false reading might spell trouble.

Table 3.1 provides a mapping of SG to PA to help with conversions. For example, if after reconstituting the concentrate you measure an SG of 1.110, you can expect the finished wine to contain *approximately* 13.6% alcohol per volume (alc./vol.) of wine if it is fermented to total dryness—that is, there is no more fermentable sugar for all practical purposes. We say "approximately" because measuring density in juice and wine is tricky; the many other solutes and the presence of carbon dioxide will affect the measurement. But don't fret over these slight inaccuracies; they are really insignificant, and even in commercial winemaking, there is often a tolerance of ±1% in alcohol declaration on labels.

A floating thermometer is used for ensuring that the juice is within the tolerable fermentation range. If the temperature falls below or jumps above the range, fermentation can become sluggish or stuck. A floating thermometer will also come in handy to ensure that the water for rehydrating yeast is within the recommended range for the yeast to become active.

The fermentation (air) lock is an essential winemaking device for protecting wine from the elements while allowing carbon dioxide gas to escape from a closed fermenter during fermentation without letting any air in (it is also a great way to monitor the speed of the fermentation). Air is wine's worst enemy and will cause spoilage if in contact with the wine for any significant period of time when the fermentation is finished. A no. 7 silicone bung is used for seating the fermentation lock on the pail lid or carboy opening.

You will be doing a lot of stirring, so get a good, long-handled, food-grade stirring spoon or paddle. The spoon or paddle portion will be used for stirring in the pail while the long-handle portion will be used for stirring in the carboy.

Winemaking involves quite a bit of racking, or transferring wine from one container to another for the purpose of separating wine from its sediment that form during fermentation and clarification procedures. For racking, you will need a *J-tube*, also known as a *racking cane*, with an anti-dregs tip and a siphoning hose. The anti-dregs tip is attached at the

Table 3.1. Specific Gravity (SG) to Potential Alcohol (PA) conversion

SG	PA (% alc./vol.)	SG	PA (% alc./vol.)
0.990	0.0	1.060	7.5
0.995	0.0	1.065	8.1
1.000	0.0	1.070	8.8
1.005	0.1	1.075	9.4
1.010	0.8	1.080	10.0
1.015	1.5	1.085	10.6
1.020	2.2	1.090	11.2
1.025	2.9	1.095	11.8
1.030	3.6	1.100	12.4
1.035	4.2	1.105	13.0
1.040	4.9	1.110	13.6
1.045	5.6	1.115	14.2
1.050	6.2	1.120	14.8
1.055	6.9	1.125	15.3

bottom of the J-tube to prevent sediment from entering the tube when siphoning wine during the various winemaking operations. The siphoning hose should be a minimum of 1.2 m (4 ft) and be equipped with a clamp to control the flow of wine while racking.

A gravy baster or wine thief will come in handy for transferring wine samples to the test cylinder to take hydrometer readings, and obviously, for the occasional tasting.

Bottles will need to be thoroughly washed, rinsed, sanitized and rinsed again; any residue in bottles is a potential source of contamination and spoilage. There is equipment that greatly eases this process. The bottle rinser, a device that attaches to the faucet, for example, on a laundry sink, is used for rinsing bottles. A bottle drainer, or bottle tree, allows you to set bottles in an inverted position to drain water or sulfite solution out. A sanitizer, a plastic container with a squirting jet that can be mounted on top of the bottle drainer, is used for sanitizing bottles with a sulfite solution.

To prepare bottles, rinse each over the bottle rinser using short bursts of water, sanitize each over the sanitizer using a sulfite solution, and then place on the bottle tree to drain. When all the bottles have been sanitized, rinse them again with fresh water and place again on the bottle tree to drain the water.

A filter unit with appropriate filter pads is used for filtering wine into a crystal clear beverage ready for bottling. This is a bit of an investment but many home winemaking shops rent these out for a nominal fee.

There are three popular units for small-batch winemaking, as shown in Fig. 3.4. The round-and-grooved plate model uses two round pads and requires an external pump. Buon Vino's Mini Jet and Superjet are fully integrated plate-and-frame models and use three pads. Pads for the two Buon Vino models are of different sizes, so be sure you purchase the right pads. The round-and-grooved plate model and Mini Jet work very well for small batches; as your production increases, the Superjet will come in very handy.

Single-use filter pads come in three grades: coarse, clarifying and fine; these are often numbered as no. 1, no. 2 and no. 3, respectively. When setting up your filtration unit, follow instructions carefully and pay particular attention to the placement of pads in the filter unit. Pads have a smooth side and a coarse side, and wine must be filtered into the coarse side and out from the smooth side. If the pads are inserted the wrong side in, the wine will not filter properly. When done with filtration, discard the pads; these are not re-usable.

For a 23-L (6-gal) batch of wine, you will need 30 clean bottles and no. 9 corks. You can use a hand or floor corker to drive corks into bottles; however, you will quickly realize that the floor model is easier to use and much more practical. Many home winemaking shops also rent this

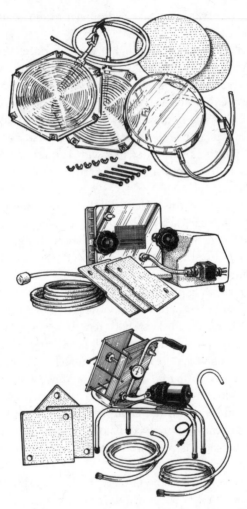

Figure 3.4. Three popular filtration units for home winemakers:
top, round-and-grooved plate model; *middle*, Buon Vino's Mini Jet model;
bottom, Buon Vino's Superjet model

out. Choose any kind of corks that you prefer or that your supplier rec-
ommends; there really isn't much of a difference if you will be drinking
the wine within twelve months or so. If you will be aging wine for 18–
24 months or more, choose an appropriate cork that will last that long.
Your supplier can recommend the right cork kind for your winemaking.
And there is no need to soak or sanitize corks if you are using corks

right out of the bag. Buy only as much as you need, and don't use corks that have been stored in opened bags for a long period of time.

CARBOYS: GLASS VERSUS PLASTIC

Until fairly recently, glass carboys were really the only practical containers for fermenting and storing wine available to home winemakers. However, glass carboys are heavy, slippery when wet, and fragile—much wine has been spilled and many people have been injured as the result of accidental breakage.

The solution? PET carboys.

Lightweight, colorless, clear, durable PET fermentation carboys were first introduced in 2003. PET plastics (also known as PETE plastics) are copolymers of polymerized polyethylene tere-phthalate and have a recycle number "1". PET belongs to the polyester family of plastics and should not be confused with toxic ortho-phthalate plasticizers such as di(2-ethylhexyl) phthalate, DEHP, and dibutyl phthalate (DBP), which are added to other types of plastics to make them flexible. It is also important to underscore that bisphenol-A (BPA), a notorious endocrine disruptor used to make polycarbonate plastics that have a recycle number of "7", has nothing to do with the manufacture of PET. Furthermore, rumors that PET containers leach toxins if they are re-used have been scientifically disproved. PET is FDA-approved and considered safe and non-toxic for food and beverage applications.

In sharp contrast to other types of plastic carboys, PET carboys do not transfer flavors to wines; are specially manufactured to have negligibly low oxygen permeability; are hydrophobic, making them easier to wash than glass; and are not damaged or stained by the washing and sanitizing agents commonly used in winemaking.

For more information on PET fermentation carboys and accessories that greatly simplify winemaking, please see http://www.better-bottle.com.

4

Making Wine

Winemaking from kits is easy and foolproof when manufacturers' instructions are followed to the letter. In general, the process involves six steps: (1) sanitization, (2) juice preparation, (3) fermentation, (4) stabilization and clarification, (5) filtration, and (6) bottling and aging.

In the following sections, step-by-step, day-by-day instructions are provided using a typical timeline for a six-week kit. Days and day ranges are approximate and representative of a six-week kit, and will vary according to your surrounding environment and the kind of kit used.

There may be some time and process variations in each of these steps from one kit to another, particularly from one manufacturer to another. Carefully read instructions provided with your kit.

And get into the habit of recording dates and all additions and measurements so that, if anything goes wrong, you can look back to try and figure out potential causes, and troubleshoot with fellow winemakers.

A handy log chart is provided in Appendix B and which can be downloaded from http://www.vehiculepress.com.

DAY 1

Refer to Fig. 4.1.

As a very first step—and this is very important—you need to sanitize *all* equipment that will come into contact with juice, any additives, or wine. This is to ensure that any microbes such as bacteria, yeasts or even molds that may have taken up residence in your equipment are adequately eradicated or inhibited; otherwise, your wine is at risk of developing spoilage problems and will be of poor quality or possibly outright spoiled.

Figure 4.1. Rinse, sanitize and rinse again all equipment

Step 1: Wash and rinse *all* equipment. Rinse *all* equipment with plenty of hot water; this includes the plastic pail to be used as the primary fermenter, the pail lid, stirring spoon, hydrometer and test cylinder, gravy baster or wine thief, thermometer, as well as containers you will be using to add water to the concentrate and to rehydrate the yeast. Make sure to scrub surfaces clear of any dirt using a clean, soft sponge or a brush with soft bristles. Use high-pressure water on the carboy, pail and other non-fragile equipment. You can use a specially formulated cleaner recommended by your winemaking supply retailer; avoid household detergents because these may leave undesirable residues that may affect the quality of the wine. After a thorough wash, rinse everything with cool water.

Step 2: Sanitize *all* equipment. This step is critical—it's the step that actually eradicates unwanted microbes. In a well-ventilated area, prepare 4 L (1 gal) of sulfite solution by dissolving 3 tbsp of potassium metabisulfite powder in 2 L (½ gal) of lukewarm water in a container with a small opening, stir thoroughly until completely dissolved, and add 2 L (½ gal) of cool water. Let the entire surface of *all* equipment make contact for several minutes with the sulfite solution. A mist sprayer—the kind used for spraying household plants—is good for this task. Save the sulfite solution in a well-stoppered glass jug for later use.

Step 3: Rinse *all* equipment with plenty of water. Rinse *all* equipment thoroughly with fresh, cool water. Let the equipment drain while you proceed to the next step.

JUICE PREPARATION

DAY 1 (continued)
Step 4: Add bentonite, if so instructed. Refer to Fig. 4.2. Before re-constituting the concentrate, you may be instructed to dissolve bentonite in a small volume of warm or hot water in the primary fermenter. This is to help the wine clarify in the later stages—a technique known as *counterfining*. Sprinkle the bentonite powder *very slowly* into the water while stirring vigorously because the bentonite clay clumps very easily. Stir thoroughly until the bentonite is well dissolved and the solution is homogeneous. If you inadvertently add all the bentonite at once and it forms one big clump, break it up with the spoon and stir, and repeat.

Figure 4.2. Adding bentonite

Figure 4.3. Reconstituting the concentrate

Step 5: Reconstitute the juice. Refer to Fig. 4.3. Open the bag of concentrate and empty the content in the primary fermenter. Rinse the bag with lukewarm water to collect any remaining concentrate and pour it in the primary fermenter. If you are making wine from concentrate where no water is to be added, for example, in an ice wine-style kit, do *not* rinse the bag—this would dilute the concentrate and not produce the desired results.

Using fresh, clean, cool water, or distilled water, add the required amount to the concentrate to bring the total volume to 23 L (6 gal), or as required for your kit. Drinking tap water is fine unless it is of poor quality or if you suspect that it is hard—that is, it has a high mineral content. Be careful not to use overly cold or hot water as you will need to have the must temperature within the ideal fermentation temperature range, as outlined below. And don't add more or less than the required amount of water, which would otherwise throw off the efficiency of ingredients to be added. Stir the must thoroughly with a stirring spoon.

Whenever possible, use soft water (i.e., water with a low mineral content) for cleaning winemaking equipment. Hard water causes scaling or the formation of limescale when minerals precipitate, and requires much more cleaning agent compared to soft water to clean effectively. You can quickly determine if your water is hard; pour a small amount of liquid soap—not detergent—in some water in a flask or closed container and shake vigorously, or alternatively, rub your hands with a bar of soap under running water. The soap should foam easily; otherwise, the water is hard. Use an alternative source of water or a water softener if your water is hard.

In preparation for inoculation, insert a floating thermometer in the must, let stand for several minutes to allow the reading to stabilize; then take a reading. The temperature should be in the range 18°C–22°C (64°F–72°F) *before* inoculating the must; if not, adjust the surrounding temperature as required to allow the must temperature to reach this range. If the temperature is outside this range and the must is inoculated, fermentation may be sluggish or perhaps not start at all

Step 6: Measure and record the SG and PA. Refer to Fig. 4.4. Measure the specific gravity (SG) of the must to ensure that it is as expected according to the kit's instructions. Place your hydrometer in the test cylinder and, using a gravy baster or wine thief, transfer must into the test cylinder to just below the top. Give the hydrometer a good spin to re-

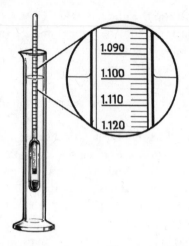

Figure 4.4. Measuring specific gravity (SG)

move any air bubbles that might still be in the must, and allow the hydrometer to stabilize; then read the SG at the bottom of the meniscus (i.e., at the surface of the must). For example, in Fig. 4.4, the SG is read as 1.100—not 1.098. Record the SG and potential alcohol (PA)—both should be within the range specified in the instructions. For example, for a dry, red table wine, the SG should be in the range 1.100–1.110 to produce 12.5%–13.5% alc./vol.

Step 7: Rehydrate and add additives. Refer to Fig. 4.5. If your kit includes other additives such as grape skins, oak chips, or dried fruits, add those now if instructed. Follow instructions for rehydrating and adding dried fruits or adding oak chips. If additives are provided in an infusion bag, do *not* remove the additives from the bag; the additives must be rehydrated in water as instructed and *then* added to the must. Stir the must thoroughly again with a stirring spoon.

Step 8: Inoculate the juice with yeast. Refer to Fig. 4.6. Inoculation is the most critical step in winemaking. Here, you will be adding the contents of the yeast packet to the must to initiate fermentation. Some manufacturers instruct to add yeast directly to the must by sprinkling the yeast pellets over the surface. This is not ideal for the yeast, and the extra time and patience to rehydrate the yeast properly is time well spent, and will give the yeast an added edge to complete the fermentation properly. As you will read later in this guide, it is much easier to spend extra time

Figure 4.5. Adding ingredients

now, properly rehydrating the yeast, rather than having to worry about a stuck fermentation later. Following is the recommended procedure to rehydrate and to add yeast to the must.

Rehydrate the contents of the yeast packet in 50 mL (1¾ fl oz) of water at a temperature in the range 35°C–40°C (95°F–105°F) for 15 minutes, or as per the manufacturer's instructions if provided on the yeast packet. Give it a quick stir with a sanitized spoon to ensure that all the yeast pellets are immersed in water. It is critical that the yeast be rehydrated within the specified temperature range and duration; otherwise, the yeast might not activate properly.

At the end of the rehydration period, stir the yeast mixture gently

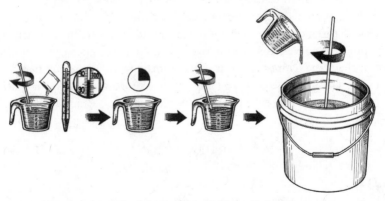

Figure 4.6. Rehydrating yeast and inoculating the must

and add it to the must. Stir the must thoroughly and place the plastic lid loosely over the pail.

It's a good idea to tag the pail with a note card or log chart containing all relevant information about the kit, kind of wine, start date and SG to better manage your production, especially if you have multiple batches going at the same time.

Step 9: Let fermentation start. Refer to Fig. 4.7. Once the must starts fermenting, it will produce gas that can cause the lid to pop if it is sealed too tightly. Alternatively, the lid can be seated tightly if it is equipped with a bung and fermentation lock. Add water in the fermentation lock to the marks indicated.

Figure 4.7. Primary fermentation

Place the primary fermenter in a relatively warm area at 18°C–22°C (64°F–72°F), ideally on a rack or table well above floor level.

Fermentation will start within 24–36 hours and last several days depending on the surrounding temperature and the kit you are using. It is also wise to monitor fermentation temperature to ensure that everything is progressing well. Insert a sanitized, floating thermometer in the must and check the temperature—it should remain within the recommended range; if not, the surrounding temperature is probably too cold, in which case you should move the pail to a warmer location or wrap a warm blanket around the pail.

FERMENTATION

DAY 2-6
Step 1: Monitor fermentation progress. Refer to Fig. 4.8. During fer-

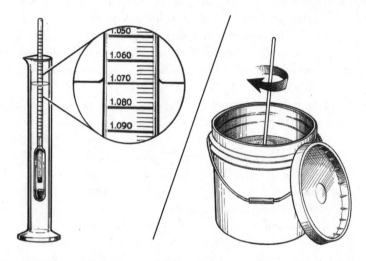

Figure 4.8. Check the SG and stir daily

mentation, measure and record the SG twice a day, once in the morning and once in the evening. At the same time, stir the fermenting wine to get the yeast back into suspension (start gently, or it may overflow the container) to favor a strong fermentation, and place the lid back on the pail.

As the wine ferments, there will be an appreciable amount of CO_2 gas produced, some of which will escape between the lid and pail and some will remain on top of the surface of the wine and provide protection against oxidation. So make sure that you lift and replace the lid as quickly as possible when needing to stir the wine or to measure the SG; you don't want to let too much CO_2 gas escape.

Let the wine ferment until the SG drops to approximately 1.030, or as instructed in your kit, being careful not to stir the wine if you have reached the target SG because you will need to rack the wine. Fermentation will now be much more subdued; this indicates the end of the primary fermentation. It is now time to transfer the wine to the secondary fermenter (the glass carboy).

DAY 7
Step 1: Wash and sanitize all equipment. Thoroughly wash, sanitize and rinse your racking tube, siphoning hose and carboy.

Step 2: Rack the wine from the pail to the carboy. Refer to Fig. 4.9. Place the carboy at floor level close to the pail on the table. Insert the anti-dregs tip at the bottom of the racking tube. Attach the top end of the racking tube to the siphoning hose, remove the lid from the pail, and gently insert the racking tube with anti-dregs tip into the wine trying not to disturb the sediment.

Hold the racking tube with one hand to avoid shaking it during the next step, and with your other hand and using your mouth, suck from the siphoning tube to draw wine from the pail; wine will start flowing down very quickly (hold your mouth close to the carboy opening to be able to transfer the hose quickly). Insert the siphoning hose into the carboy, place the racking tube diagonally from the bottom rim of the pail to the top, and rack all the wine from the pail.

If you would rather avoid siphoning using your mouth to avoid contaminating the wine, there are various siphoning starter devices on the market that greatly simplify this procedure. Alternatively, you can fill the flexible part of the siphoning tube with water by immersing it in a pail of clean water; slowly insert the racking tube into the wine pail while holding the siphoning tube level so that water does not flow out; and

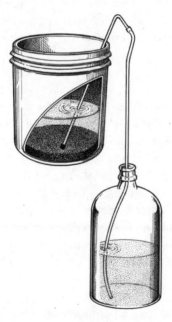

Figure 4.9. Racking the wine to the secondary fermenter

then, quickly drop the tube into the carboy to get gravity to start the flow of wine.

Stop siphoning when all the wine has been transferred. It's okay to transfer some sediment; actually some manufacturers instruct to rack all the sediment to the carboy. Sediment is rich in yeast, which will favor a good fermentation. Discard all leftover sludge.

Note that you will end up with less than 23 L (6 gal) because of loss from sediment and from racking. Don't worry about the headspace in the carboy at this stage since the wine is still fermenting, and the fermentation gas will displace air out of the carboy (and protect the wine) without letting any air in once you place a fermentation lock on the carboy. You will also need the extra headspace for stirring the wine in later steps.

Step 3: Let fermentation run its course. Refer to Fig. 4.10. Pour some water into the fermentation lock up to the line indicated and insert it in a no. 7 bung. Seat the bung and fermentation lock assembly onto the carboy, and set the carboy aside in a relatively warm area at 18°C–22°C (64°F–72°F), away from strong light sources and vibrations, to let the secondary (alcoholic) fermentation run its course. You will see some slow bubbling through the water and up the fermentation lock; the bubbling will subdue as fermentation dies off.

Transfer the log chart from the pail to the carboy and update all relevant information.

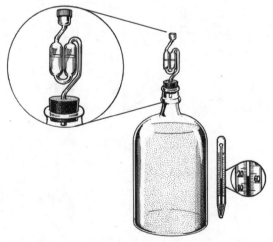

Figure 4.10. Let fermentation run its course in a carboy secured with a bung and fermentation lock.

Wash, sanitize, rinse and store away your primary fermentation equipment.

DAY 8–14

Let the wine finish fermenting—you can visually verify this when there is no more bubbling. The wine will still be fermenting for a short while but will be barely visible. Let the wine stand to let fermentation finish off completely and to allow solids in suspension to sediment to the bottom of the carboy.

You are ready to rack the wine when the SG has reached 0.995 or lower, or as indicated in your kit's instructions. Depending on the style of wine you are making, you may be instructed to rack at a different SG, so be sure to pay careful attention to instructions.

STABILIZATION AND CLARIFICATION

DAY 14
Step 1: Confirm end of fermentation. Refer to Fig. 4.11. Using your (sanitized) hydrometer and test cylinder, measure and record the SG—it should read 0.995 or lower for a dry wine, or as instructed in your kit. If the SG reads higher than the final target SG, the wine has not finished fermenting; replace the bung and fermentation lock on the carboy

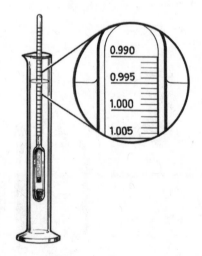

Figure 4.11. The SG should read 0.995 or lower, or as indicated in your kit, to confirm end of fermentation.

and let stand for another day or two, or until the SG drops to the final target SG or lower.

> WARNING: Do *not* proceed with the next step until your wine has completely finished fermenting and the SG is at the final target SG or lower; otherwise, the wine will not finish as expected and can start refermenting, possibly even once bottled. If you are unsure, it's always safer to let the wine settle for a couple of extra days or more than to rush the process.

Once fermentation has completed, you are ready to start stabilizing and clarifying the wine. Some kits require that the wine be racked to another carboy while others require that the sediment be left in the wine. If you are instructed to rack the wine, some manufacturers will instruct you to rack the wine from the carboy into another carboy—or a pail if working with only one carboy—and *then* to add the packet of potassium metabisulfite to stabilize and protect the wine from oxidation and spoilage bacteria and yeasts. A better alternative is to add the sulfite (as a solution) into the receiving carboy before racking; that way, the wine is protected as it is being racked.

Step 2: Sanitize all your equipment. Rinse, sanitize and rinse again *all* your equipment as shown in Fig. 4.1.

Step 3: Rack, stabilize and degas wine. Refer to Fig. 4.12 and Fig. 4.13.

> NOTE: Manufacturers may instruct to add the packet of sulfite directly to the wine; it is recommended to dissolve the sulfite powder in a little water because it may not dissolve properly in wine.

Dissolve the content of the sulfite (potassium metabisulfite) packet into a little water and stir thoroughly until well dissolved. Pour the sulfite solution to the bottom of the carboy (or pail) by letting the solution drop down the wall of the carboy. Repeat with the packet of potassium sorbate, if instructed to do so at this time; some kits will instruct to add this toward the end.

Next, rack the wine into the carboy (or pail), as shown in Fig. 4.12.

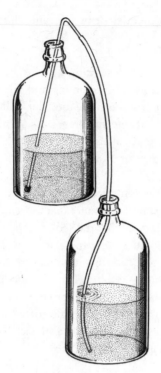

Figure 4.12. Racking from one carboy to another

Figure 4.13. Add sulfite and sorbate and stir vigorously

You may want to wedge up one side of the carboy (the one containing wine) and seat the J-tube at the opposite side to minimize wine loss during racking. Insert the siphoning hose all the way down the receiving carboy or let the wine flow down the side of the carboy to minimize aeration, which could otherwise hasten oxidation.

Rack all the wine to the carboy being careful not to draw in sediment when nearing the bottom of the carboy. If you have racked well, losses will be limited to the volume of sediment and the carboy will be nearly full. Do not top up at this time since you now need to stir the wine and you will need that extra headspace. Discard the sediment and clean the carboy with fresh water.

Insert the long-handle portion of the stirring spoon or paddle and, using a circular wrist action, stir the wine for several minutes to dissipate any residual gas left in the wine, which will otherwise make the wine fizzy, and to thoroughly mix in the sulfite and sorbate solutions. Keep stirring until there is no more fizz, which would otherwise indicate that gas is still dissolved in the wine, and you need to get it out. Optionally, you can use a stirring stem and electric drill, as shown in Fig. 4.14, to make this work easier since it requires quite a bit of arm and wrist work. And be sure to first sanitize the stirring stem. Use caution with the stirring stem as it will create a lot of foam, which can spill out of the carboy. Use short bursts of stirring to gauge if the fizz is dissipating; do not overdo this step as you do not want to start introducing too much oxygen into the wine.

If your kit requires you to add a sweetener or other additives to achieve the desired style of wine, do so now as instructed.

Step 4: Start clarification process. Refer to Fig. 4.15. Prepare the fining agents as per instructions, add to the wine, and stir thoroughly. If the fining agents provided with the kit include kieselsol, and gelatin or chitosan, you must *add the kieselsol first and then the gelatin or chitosan*; the wine will not fine properly if you reverse the order. You can stir some more at this point to further degas the wine.

If you racked the wine into a plastic pail—that is, if you don't have a second carboy—rack again, back into the cleaned carboy.

At this point, there should be no more than approximately 4 cm (1½ inches) of headspace. If there is too much headspace, wine will oxidize prematurely or potentially spoil if spoilage bacteria or yeasts become active, and so, you will need to top up the wine.

Figure 4.14. Using a stirring stem with a drill to degas wine

Figure 4.15. Adding fining agents to wine

You have several options to top up the carboy and reduce headspace. You can either add a small amount of similar wine (purchased commercially) if the headspace is significant, or you can add a little water, or carefully drop in some sanitized marbles to increase the overall volume in the carboy. If the headspace is significant, it is not recommended to add water, which would otherwise dilute the wine (i.e., alcohol, body, aromas and flavors).

Reattach the bung and fermentation lock on the carboy. Place the carboy in a cooler area at a temperature in the range 13°C–18°C (55°F–65°F).

DAY 14–41

Let the wine clarify as instructed and, optionally, you can rack the wine to another carboy after two weeks. At the end of the fining period, the wine will be completely clear without any traces of cloudiness. You should see objects clearly on the other side of the carboy. If there is any visible cloudiness, wait until it completely settles out.

DAY 42

Step 1: Rack the wine. Once the wine is crystal clear, you are ready to rack the wine to a clean and sanitized carboy, as shown in Fig. 4.12. Follow the sanitizing and racking instructions above, being careful not to siphon any sediment.

Step 2: Degas and bottle wine if not filtering. Most often, four- to six-week kits will instruct you to filter the wine: If so, follow the instructions in the following section; otherwise, you can proceed with bottling.

Before filtering, taste the wine to make sure that it is not fizzy. If there is still residual gas, stir the wine vigorously with the long handle of the stirring spoon or paddle until there is no more foaming.

FILTRATION

DAY 42 (continued)

Step 3: Filter the wine. Once the wine has completely cleared and has been completely degassed, you are ready to filter and bottle. These two operations should be performed the same day. You will need a second sanitized carboy for filtering; you could always use the plastic pail used as the primary fermenter but the wine would be overly exposed to air.

Depending on your filtration equipment, your setup will be one of the two shown in Fig. 4.16. The setup in Fig. 4.16 (top) is ideal for small batches of 23 L (6 gal) whereas the setup in Fig. 4.16 (bottom) can be used for larger or multiple batches. The setup you choose may also depend on what your home winemaking supply shop has available if you are renting a filter unit.

Before filtering, determine what rating of filter pads you will need for your wine. In general, wine should be successively filtered through no. 1 (coarse) pads followed by no. 2 (clarifying) and then no. 3 (fine) pads to achieve optimal clarity. Multiple filtration operations, which can hasten oxidation, should be evaluated against the clarity of the wine—there is always a trade-off. And never combine filter pads of different ratings in the same filtration run in the filter unit to reduce the number of operations; this will not work and may compromise filtration efficiency and quality.

In the case of white wines that have been adequately fined, you can usually achieve maximum clarity by using no. 3 pads only; if in doubt, use no. 2 pads first.

In the case of red wines that have been adequately fined, you can

Figure 4.16. Filtration setups: *top*, suction-type system; *bottom*, plate-and-frame system

usually achieve maximum clarity by using no. 2 pads followed by no. 3 pads; if in doubt, use no. 1 pads first. You may find that the wine is very clear even after the no. 2 filtration.

It is recommended to filter wine at a cool temperature, for example, at cellar temperature, at around 13°C (55°F), for a more effective filtration operation.

Set up your filtration system according to one of the configurations in Fig. 4.16 based on your equipment. Saturate the pads with clean water and let any excess drip before inserting the pads in the filtration unit. Assemble the system as per the manufacturer's instructions. Be sure to position, align and secure pads properly, particularly if the pads have holes that channel wine in and out of the system, so that the rough side faces the inlet. In Fig. 4.16 (top), the rough surface of the pads should face each other when the filter unit is assembled. In Fig. 4.16 (bottom), the rough surface of all pads should face toward the pump. In either setup, tighten the plates-and-pads assembly to minimize wine leakage during filtration.

Next, sanitize the entire filtration system, including the pads, before filtering wine. Fill a carboy with fresh, cool water, turn on the pump, and collect the water in the receiving carboy and discard. This operation ensures that all components are rinsed properly and removes any carton flavor from the pads, which could otherwise be imparted to the wine. When you first start the pump in the setup of Fig. 4.16 (top), lock the control clip on the outlet tube on the upper plate to restrict flow of water into it so that the filter unit fills bottom-up. When the filter unit is full, open the clip. When filtering is completed, lock the clip again to drain any remaining water out of the filter unit. There is no control clip to worry about in the setup of Fig. 4.16 (bottom).

Repeat the above procedure with approximately 10 L (2½ gal) of sulfite solution to sanitize the entire system. Then flush the system using approximately 10 L of fresh water to rinse out any sulfite solution remaining in the filtration system. The system is now ready for wine filtering.

Double-check that everything is set up properly and then proceed with filtering the wine according to your system's setup.

As you start filtering wine, the first half to one liter (⅛–¼ gal) of liquid to pass through the system will contain mostly water. The volume of diluted wine depends on the amount of water left in the unit during the flushing operation. Discard the diluted wine by filtering it out to a waste container and return the outlet tube to the receiving carboy when the wine seems undiluted.

If the filtration system is equipped with a pressure gauge, monitor the filtering pressure, and stop the pump and replace the clogged pads if the manufacturer's recommended maximum pressure is reached. Typically, an increase in pressure indicates that the pads are clogging, which will cause the filtering to leak and spray wine. Once the pump is turned on and filtering has started, do not turn the pump off-on or interrupt the operation by any other means; this will greatly decrease filtering efficiency and may affect the clarity of the wine.

When filtration has completed, discard the filter pads, rinse and sanitize the entire system again with water and a sulfite solution, as outlined above for the filter set-up phase.

Leave the wine in the carboy, with a bung, while you set up for bottling.

If you intend to age the wine for a prolonged period of time, for example, more than six months, add more sulfite before bottling to prevent premature spoilage. This may not be mentioned in the instructions but is highly recommended. For a 23-L (6-gal) batch, dissolve approximately ¼ tsp of sulfite powder or three crushed Campden tablets in a little water, add the solution to the wine in the carboy, and stir thoroughly. Proceed with bottling immediately.

If you intend to bulk age the wine in the carboy, you will need to add a little bit of sulfite every 2–3 months: simply dissolve a pinch of powder, or the equivalent of the tip of a teaspoon, in a little water, add to the wine, and stir well.

TO FILTER OR NOT TO FILTER?

There is a misconception that filtering wine is not good, that it strips the wine of color, aromas, flavors, and all sorts of important compounds. The reality is that almost all wines are filtered, and only the super-premium (read, very expensive) wines aren't. Labels on super-premium wines will often indicate that the wine is unfiltered, which is a clever marketing tactic to connote superior quality, and that they are expected to throw deposits. But most consumers do not like (or do not understand why) wine to throw deposits. It's those deposits that are being filtered, and so you are not really stripping the wine of anything, unless you filter excessively.

As a general rule, you should always filter your wines, particularly early drinking ones. If you intend to age the wine for 18–24 months or more, you can fine lightly, forego filtration, and, instead, rack the wine every 3–6 months. The wine will turn out very clear although it will still throw some light to moderate deposits depending on the style of wine. Highly tannic wines will throw more deposits because tannins act as a fining agent.

BOTTLING AND AGING

DAY 42 (continued)

Step 4: Bottle wine. At long last, time to bottle that precious wine!

As with any other winemaking process, the first step here is to clean and sanitize bottles. You will need 30 bottles for a 23-L (6-gal) kit. Set up your bottle tree with the sanitizer installed on the top and half-filled with sulfite solution. Have the corker and corks ready. Buy a new bag of corks; that way, they won't need to be sanitized. An old, opened bag may have become contaminated with airborne microbes that could compromise the quality of the corks and thus the bottled wine, and potentially cause spoilage.

Install a bottle rinser on a faucet over a laundry sink and open the hot-water tap and the cold tap just slightly—a hot-water rinse is more effective. Thoroughly rinse each bottle over the bottle rinser. Allow the water to splash vigorously inside the bottle, but only momentarily, and repeat two or three times; this is more effective than keeping the water running and allowing it to accumulate inside the bottle. Then sanitize each bottle by pressing it over the squirt jet on the sanitizer, and repeat two or three times. Place the bottle at the bottom of the bottle tree to allow it to drain completely. Repeat this procedure for all bottles. When all bottles have been cleaned and sanitized, optionally, you can rinse the bottles again to remove any trace of sulfite. The little sulfite than remains in bottles is not a problem (actually, it will further protect the wine); however, if your sulfite solution is strong, it may leave a detectable smell in the wine.

Set the carboy with wine on a counter or some location above floor level and gather all bottles on the floor, close to the carboy. Insert a sanitized racking tube and siphoning hose with a locking clip (to start and stop flow) in the carboy and suck the air from it to start drawing wine into the siphoning hose. Alternatively, you can use a bottle filler wand, as shown in Fig. 4.17, which greatly simplifies the bottling operation. There are other devices that greatly simplify this task and reduce bottling time; consult your home winemaking supply shop.

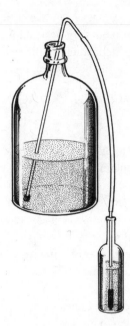

Figure 4.17. Using a filler wand to fill bottles

As wine begins to flow, insert the hose or wand inside a bottle and fill to 5 cm (2 in) from the top. If using a filler wand, simply allow the wine to reach the top of the bottle, and then lift the filler wand to stop the flow. The wine level will drop back down to the right level. Leave approximately 1.5 cm (½ in) of headspace between the wine and cork.

Repeat this bottling operation until all the wine is bottled. Immediately cork all bottles, as shown in Fig. 4.18. Insert a cork in the corker, set a bottle on the round plate making sure that the mouth of the bottle comes properly seated under the corker opening, and then simply depress the corker to insert the cork in the bottle. Corks do not need to be soaked; a good corker will drive a dry cork without any problems.

Leave bottles upright for several days to allow the cork to expand back to seal the bottle properly, and then store bottles upside down or sideways in a cool cellar.

Optionally, you can dress bottles with labels and capsules. You can either purchase labels—there are labels for every kind and style of wine—or make your own on your computer. Print labels on pressure-sensitive paper (the peel-and-stick kind) or on glue-backed paper, which you will need to wet with a sponge or some other device before apply-

Figure 4.18. Corking bottles

ing on the bottle. Do some tests with various kinds of paper and glue to make sure that you will be able to easily remove labels once you empty bottles and reuse them for your next batch.

Capsules come in a plethora of colors and designs manufactured from PVC (a thermoplastic polymer) that shrinks when heat is applied. To shrink a capsule, use a heat gun, or use a continuous-boil kettle as shown in Fig. 4.19. Apply the heat evenly with the gun or move the cap-

Figure 4.19. Shrinking a PVC capsule

sule steadily into the steam to ensure that the capsule shrinks evenly.

Lay away bottles in your cellar. You can start drinking wine as soon as bottled; however, it will greatly improve with some aging, particularly with premium kits. A minimum of 6 months of aging is recommended for white wines and 6–12 months for reds. This cellaring period also allows the wine to "settle down" and to recover from all the handling from filtration and bottling—a condition referred to as *bottle shock*—which may alter the character of the wine, if only for a short period of time.

5

Dealing With Problems

Making wine from kits is very simple and trouble-free when manufacturers' instructions are followed to the letter; however, unexpected results or problems can arise. A fermentation is, after all, a microbiological process, not an absolutely perfect transformation.

Here, we examine the most common winemaking problems encountered by novice winemakers and how to correct those; but not all can be fixed, and so, the best cure is prevention. In many cases, the root cause is rushed winemaking, poor sanitation, or an inadequate fermentation environment, which can all easily be avoided.

FERMENTATION IS SLUGGISH OR STUCK
A sluggish or stuck fermentation is a condition where there is little or no yeast activity, whether it never started or has ceased, and yeast is no longer able to convert sugar into alcohol.

With kits, this happens most often when the fermentation temperature is below or above the yeast's recommended temperature range specified in the instructions, or when the yeast has not been adequately prepared.

Before pitching the yeast in the must, set the surrounding room temperature to the recommended range in the instructions and allow the must to stabilize at that temperature; you may need to warm up the room the evening before starting your kit. Maintain this temperature through-out fermentation and you will not have any problems.

If the must and surrounding temperatures are within the recom-mended range but fermentation is sluggish or becomes stuck, the yeast is struggling or has stopped doing its work because it was not prepared properly. Yeast has to be rehydrated within the recommended tempera-ture range and duration to become active. Stir the wine twice a day dur-ing fermentation to get the yeast back into suspension. If fermentation has become completely stuck, buy a packet of equivalent yeast as the one supplied in the kit, rehydrate as instructed, and add to the juice or wine; fermentation will restart within 24 hours.

WINE IS REFERMENTING IN BOTTLES

Wine that referments in bottles is the result of an incomplete fermenta-tion because of sugar still present in the wine at bottling time. This will cause corks to pop or, in the worst case, bottles to explode if the glass is structurally weak.

The only viable solution is to uncork all bottles and pour the wine back into a carboy to let the fermentation complete. If the SG is still fairly high, add a fresh culture of rehydrated yeast to ensure that the wine ferments completely without any problems. Only bottle when the hy-drometer reads 0.995 or less. Add fresh doses of sulfite and sorbate at the end of fermentation before bottling again.

WINE IS SWEET, NOT DRY

A dry-style wine that has perceptible sweetness—there is unfermented, residual sugar in the wine—is very simply the result of an incomplete fer-mentation, either because of a sluggish or stuck fermentation that has gone unnoticed, or because fermentation progress was not monitored and you proceeded to stabilize the wine too early.

It is probably best to drink the wine as is, and chalk this one up as a lesson learned. If you are adamant on a dry wine, uncork all bottles and pour the wine back into a carboy. Add a fresh culture (possibly two pack-ets) of a strong fermenting yeast (see Chapter 6) as well as yeast nutri-ents to the wine to restart fermentation and let it complete to dryness. Your ability to restart fermentation depends on the concentration of sul-fite in the wine; there is a high probability that you may not be able to restart it. Only bottle when the hydrometer reads 0.995 or less. Add fresh doses of sulfite and sorbate at the end of fermentation before bottling again.

Alternatively, you can blend the wine with one having fairly high acidity; this will reduce the perception of sweetness, making the wine more palatable. Refer to Chapter 6 for more information on blending wines.

Get into the habit of measuring fermentation with your hydrometer twice a day—once in the morning and once in the evening. If fermentation is not progressing as expected, you will be able to quickly identify the problem and to take immediate corrective action, increasing your chances of getting the fermentation to complete.

WINE IS TOO DRY

A wine that is too dry is more of a perception or preference; it is a result of the wine acidity being quite high, and there is not sufficient residual sugar to mask it, at least not for your taste. This may not be a "real" problem if the kit was meant to produce a dry-style wine; but it is a real problem for you if you did not expect that much acidity.

The problem is easily remedied by adding some sugar until you reach the right balance that appeals to your taste. Add sugar as a solution, because it is easier to control the required quantity. Additions are done at bottling time.

First perform bench trials with varying levels of sugar additions to determine the right amount of sugar to add for your taste. Prepare a 10% sugar solution by dissolving 10 g (approximately 2 tsp) of sugar in sufficient, lightly boiled water to prepare 100 mL (3½ fl oz) of solution.

Prepare a few tasting glasses each with 30 mL (1 fl oz) of the "acidic" wine. Label the first glass as "control"—don't add any sugar to this one; it will be used for comparison purposes—and label all other glasses as 1, 2, 3, etc. With a syringe, measure out a small volume of sugar solution, for example, 1 mL, and add to glass no. 1; repeat with, for example, 5 mL of sugar solution and add to glass no. 2, and repeat with 10 mL and add to glass no. 3.

Taste, assess and compare all samples from each glass, including the control sample. If you determine that, for example, 1 mL is too little and 5 mL is too much, repeat the test with sugar solution volume additions between 2 and 4 mL, for example, and until you reach the level that appeals to your taste. For example, if you have determined that you need 3.0 mL to balance your 30 mL sample of wine, then you need 10 g (0.35 oz) of sugar per liter (¼ gal) of wine, or 230 g (8 oz) for your 23-L (6-gal) batch.

Before adding the sugar to your batch, ensure that the wine is fully stabilized with sulfite as well as potassium sorbate—because you will be adding sugar, you need to protect the wine against renewed fermentation. Add 2–4 g of potassium sorbate to your 23-L (6-gal) batch by first dissolving the pellets in some water, and stir thoroughly. Then, completely dissolve the required volume of sugar in a small volume of warm wine, add the sugar solution to the wine batch, and stir thoroughly.

Alternatively, you can blend the wine with one having some residual sugar and perceptible sweetness, which will reduce dryness and make the wine more palatable. Refer to Chapter 6 for more information on blending wines.

WINE IS CLOUDY

A kit wine that is cloudy is the result of improper racking or clarification—either fining or filtering—or both, assuming that fermentation has completed. Wine will be cloudy as long as it is fermenting.

If the wine has *not* been fined or filtered but is cloudy, allow it to stand for a couple of days more in a cool area; you should notice a gradual clearing. If cooler temperatures are available, chill the wine to hasten clarification. Once it is completely clear, proceed with the fining and filtering operations as instructed. Never rush the racking operation; give the wine time to clear on its own.

If the wine has been fined or filtered or both and is still cloudy, allow it to stand for a couple of days more; you should notice a gradual clearing. Once it is completely clear, filter the wine with coarse pads and then again with clarifying pads; optionally, you can filter once more with fine pads for a brilliant wine.

Follow your kit's instructions on the timing of racking operations, addition of fining agents, and filtration. Maintain temperature within the recommended range since it will otherwise affect the clarification period or efficiency. And never disturb sediment at the bottom of a carboy while racking; getting sediment back into suspension will cause the wine to become cloudy and throw sediment in the bottle.

WINE IS FIZZY

A fizzy wine is the result of CO_2 gas still dissolved in the wine and which has not been degassed adequately before bottling.

If the fizzy wine is still in a carboy and has not been bottled, first let the carboy warm up to room temperature to reduce solubility of the gas and ease degassing, then stir the wine vigorously with the long handle of your stirring spoon or, better yet, with a stirring stem mounted on a drill, until there is no perceptible gas when you taste the wine. If there is a lot of gas still dissolved, you will need to let the wine rest a little and then stir vigorously again. Taste the wine to make sure there is no perceptible gas before you bottle.

If the fizzy wine is bottled—but it is dry—you can drink the wine if it is acceptable; otherwise, you will need to uncork all bottles and pour the wine back into a carboy. Stir the wine vigorously with the long handle of your stirring spoon until there is no perceptible gas before bottling again.

WINE SMELLS AND TASTES "GRAPEY"

Very young wine—only days or weeks after it is "finished" (i.e., ready to drink)—will smell and taste "grapey," akin to freshly squeezed grape juice and unlike that promised Bordeaux-style red.

Wine is a very complex beverage that needs time to evolve to its full potential, even a four-week kit wine. There is nothing wrong with the wine; it simply needs a little time. There are no hard and fast rules on how long to age wines before drinking; but, as a guideline, try aging whites for six months, a little longer for reds.

To learn how wines change over time, taste wine at bottling and again after three, six, nine and twelve months, and compare flavors, aromas and overall quality. Keep notes from each tasting and compare.

WINE SMELLS OF ROTTEN EGGS (H_2S)

A stinky smell of rotten eggs or even burnt rubber is the result of the presence of sulfide compounds, specifically, hydrogen sulfide (H_2S), in must or wine. Since kit manufacturers go to great lengths to ensure quality and provenance of their grape and juice as well as in their production process, this problem is usually the result of poor or careless winemaking.

Common causes of H_2S in wine include excessive use of sulfite, yeast nutrient deficiency, extended contact with gross (heavy) lees, and extreme, stressful fermentation temperatures. To avoid any of these problems, only add as much sulfite as needed (refer to Chapter 6), add yeast nutrients if provided with the kit, rack wine in timely fashion after primary fermentation so that the wine is not allowed to be in contact with the lees for an extended period of time, and respect the prescribed fermentation temperature range.

Your ability to correct the problem depends on the extent of H_2S concentration. If H_2S is barely detectable, there is a good chance that it can be eliminated by aerating the wine, such as by racking. This has the drawback of accelerating oxidation and has to be assessed against the severity of the problem.

If H_2S is quite noticeable, do not aerate the wine, because it can further compound the problem and make it irreversible by transforming H_2S into mercaptans and disulfides—foul-smelling compounds that cause wine to spoil and which is best dumped down the sewer.

Alternatively, you can call upon a wine expert or lab that can treat your wine with a dilute copper sulfate solution. Do *not* try this on your own; leave it to an expert experienced in the handling of such chemicals. Detailed instructions are provided in *Techniques in Home Winemaking* (Véhicule Press, 2008) on using copper sulfate as well as on alternative treatments.

SOMETHING HAS GONE TERRIBLY WRONG

You have made a great batch of wine from that promising premium kit, but then, after a short aging period, you discover one or more serious flaws, some of which make the wine unpleasant or downright undrinkable. What has gone so wrong?

The all-too-common culprit is oxidation, either because of a poor topping regimen or faulty equipment, or perhaps insufficient use of sulfite (this should not be a problem if you have followed your kits' instructions properly). The root cause is oxidation—that is, the wine has been overly exposed to air. The problem will manifest itself in one of several ways depending on the extent of oxidation. The wine will start taking on brownish hues, best seen around the rim of the wine when the glass is held at an angle, and smell like a sherry-style wine. If acetic acid bacteria are allowed to reach the wine, for example, if fruit flies have taken up residence in your wine, it will take on a vinegary smell. In the worst case, if some airborne spoilage yeasts reach the wine, a slimy, whitish film will form on the surface causing the wine to spoil.

None of the above problems can be cured satisfactorily, and the wine is best poured down the drain, quite unfortunately. Do not be tempted to blend the wine with a perfectly good wine to try and mask the problem—the result will be a mediocre wine now contaminated with spoilage.

Evidently, the best cure is prevention. Be sure to use sulfite adequately and when instructed to add, top up carboys to avoid too much headspace; and verify that all your equipment is in perfect condition, and regularly check fermentation locks have not run dry. Check for hairline cracks on joints on fermentation locks, especially old ones, which can serendipitously allow air to enter the carboy.

6
Advanced Topics

This chapter covers advanced topics including: choosing yeast strains, chaptalizing, managing acidity, managing sulfite, stabilizing wine against cold temperatures, carrying out malolactic fermentation, and blending.

CHOOSING YEASTS

The role of yeast goes well beyond that of converting sugar into alcohol. Yeast is also responsible for imparting aromas, flavors and volume, and when well matched to specific varietals, wine can fully exhibit all its organoleptic qualities and varietal character. By selecting different yeast strains, you can create wines with different aroma and flavor profiles.

Kits are often packaged with a yeast strain that ensures trouble-free fermentation—and that is the main consideration from manufacturers—and is often not identified. Some will provide a yeast strain that best achieves the desired style of the kit; but this is more the exception than the norm.

By doing a little research on home winemaking yeast strains available on the market, you can further improve the quality and style of your wine by choosing an appropriate yeast that enhances fermentation. Following is a list of the most popular yeasts and their characteristics. Full product documentation is available from yeast manufacturers' websites listed.

Here, we only describe those yeast products packaged as dry pellets in 5-g packets; these are the kind supplied with kits because they are stable. Yeast products are also available in liquid format, although they have a shorter shelf-life. For more information on liquid cultures, consult http://www.whitelabs.com or http://www.wyeastlab.com.

LALVIN YEASTS

EC-1118: This *S. bayanus* strain is considered the workhorse of wine yeasts because it provides for a quick, trouble-free fermentation in a wide range of environments, making it most suitable for kit winemaking where consistently predictable results are required. It is recommended for restarting a stuck or sluggish fermentation, for fermenting sugar-rich musts for making sweet wine, and for bottle fermentation in sparkling winemaking.

Bourgovin RC 212: As the name implies, this *S. cerevisiae* yeast strain is particularly recommended for crafting Burgundian-style Pinot Noir. In general, it is recommended for making full-bodied reds where full tannin extraction and color stabilization are desired.

K1-V1116: This yeast strain is the strongest fermenter of the species *S. cerevisiae*, and can ferment under difficult conditions, making it suitable for kit winemaking. It is recommended for restarting a stuck or sluggish fermentation and for fermenting sugar-rich musts for making sweet wine.

71B-1122: This *S. cerevisiae* yeast strain is recommended for making young wines not meant for aging and when varietal character and fruity aromas are desired. Rosé (blush) wines, young reds, and whites with residual sugar, benefit most from this strain.

ICV-D47: The properties of this *S. cerevisiae* yeast strain make it most suitable for rosé (blush) wines and whites with residual sugar.

Additional information on LALVIN wine yeasts can be found at http://www.lalvinyeast.com/strains.asp.

RED STAR YEASTS

Premier Cuvée: This *S. bayanus* yeast strain is equivalent to the LALVIN EC-1118 yeast strain described above. It is recommended for restarting a stuck or sluggish fermentation, for fermenting sugar-rich musts for making sweet wine, and for bottle fermentation in sparkling winemaking.

Pasteur Champagne: In spite of its name, this *S. bayanus* yeast strain is not intended—nor is it recommended—for sparkling winemaking but rather for dry white wines. It is also recommended for restarting a stuck or sluggish fermentation.

Pasteur Red: This *S. cerevisiae* yeast strain is recommended for making full-bodied red wines where varietal fruit flavors and complex aromas are desired.

Côte des Blancs: The properties of this *S. cerevisiae* yeast strain make it most suitable for rosé (blush) wines and whites with residual sugar.

Montrachet: This *S. cerevisiae* yeast strain is recommended for full-bodied, intense-color red wines, and white wines. Its only drawback is that it can produce detectable levels of hydrogen sulfide (H_2S), responsible for a rotten-egg smell. See Chapter 5 for more information on hydrogen sulfide (H_2S).

Additional information on RED STAR wine yeasts can be found at http://www.fermentis.com.

CHAPTALIZATION

Chaptalization is the practice of adding sugar to must or wine to either increase the potential alcohol content or to add sweetness to a finished wine. Remember that the amount of sugar fermented determines the amount of alcohol produced and, as a rule of thumb, 17 g of sugar per liter (2¼ oz per gallon) will raise the alcohol content by 1% alc./vol.

Only chaptalize kits that specifically instruct to add sugar, otherwise you risk running into problems either fermenting the juice or, worse yet, the bottled wine will start refermenting.

Kits are designed and manufactured to provide predictably consistent results. The most important component in the kit is yeast, which has been selected to perform according to the "chemistry" of the juice. Adding sugar to must could potentially inhibit the yeast, resulting in a stuck or sluggish fermentation.

In a finished wine, adding sugar before bottling for a sweeter-style wine can cause bottle refermentation and corks to pop or, worse yet, bottles to explode. When wine is bottled, there is always a small population of yeast cells that could start feeding on sugar and restart fermentation. In commercial winemaking, wines are sterile filtered to remove unwanted yeast; but this requires specialized equipment and techniques. In home winemaking, the only option is to add potassium sorbate before adding sugar. If the kit is for a sweeter-style wine, potassium sorbate should already be provided with the kit additives.

MANAGING TOTAL ACIDITY (TA) AND pH

Kits are designed and manufactured to produce balanced and stable wines. Balanced wines have levels of alcohol, acidity, astringency and sweetness, that come together to provide a pleasurable beverage. Stable wines are better protected against microbiological effects that could otherwise spoil wine.

Acidity and pH are two important parameters in wine balance and stability. Acidity, or more precisely, *total titratable acidity (TA)*, is a measure of acid concentration and provides reds with structure, and freshness in whites, while pH is a measure of the strength of the acids and provides an indication of the wine's stability—the higher the pH, the less stable the wine and the more sulfite is needed for protection, and yet the less effective sulfite is.

Kit wines are balanced and do not need any adjustment to acidity or pH. If you are interested in getting acquainted with and measuring these parameters, you can purchase an easy-to-use total titratable acidity kit and pH meter.

Measure TA and pH before the start and at the end of fermentation, and just before bottling (any cold stabilization procedure would have re-

Table 6.1. Recommended TA and pH ranges for different kinds of must and wine

Kind of wine	TA range for must (g/L)	TA range for wine (g/L)	pH range for must and wine
Dry white	7.0–9.0	5.0–7.5	3.1–3.4
Dry red	6.0–8.0	4.0–5.5	3.3–3.6
Sweet white	7.5–9.0	5.5–7.5	3.1–3.2

duced the acidity). Table 6.1 provides some guidelines for TA and pH in musts and wines. TA is measured in g/L or as a percentage where each 1 g/L equals 0.1%, and pH is unitless. Water has a theoretical pH value of 7; anything less is acidic, anything higher is basic (alkaline).

And here is an important piece of advice: Do *not* adjust acidity simply for the sake of "hitting" the target range; but rather, let your taste dictate what adjustments, if any, are required. Ultimately, wine is about taste and balance, so let your palate guide you. In his book *Le Goût du Vin*, Émile Peynaud, forefather of modern enology, presents some simple guiding principles to help you achieve great balance: High-alcohol wines can assimilate higher acidity, where more freshness is desired; however, bitterness and acidity reinforce each other, and therefore in reds, aim for lower acidity in very tannic wines..

As a guideline, 1 g of tartaric acid will increase TA of 1 L of must or wine by 1 g/L, or 0.1%, or 4 g (0.13 oz) in 1 gal.

It gets trickier if you need to reduce acidity, although this should typically never be required for wine from a kit since the manufacturer has ensured a proper balance for the style of wine. Slight corrections are best addressed by adding sugar to balance the acidity, as outlined in the section on *Wine is Too Dry* in Chapter 5.

If you need to reduce acidity beyond a slight adjustment, your best solution is to use potassium bicarbonate because it reduces tartaric acid at approximately the same rate of addition. To reduce TA by 1 g/L, you simply need to add 1 g/L of potassium bicarbonate—dissolve the powder in a small volume of wine, not water, first. Again, perform bench trials to determine what works best before treating the whole batch. Some literature may recommend calcium carbonate as an alternative product to reduce acidity; it is not recommended because it imparts an unappealing earthy taste to wine. When adding potassium bicarbonate to a small part of wine, do not be alarmed—the wine will change color quite drastically; this will not affect the total wine color once added.

Amelioration is another method of reducing acidity that is recommended in literature. The technique simply involves adding water to wine. It is ironic that it is known as *amelioration* as the technique also dilutes color, aromas and flavors, which do not improve wine. For this reason, this is generally not a good practice except for very small additions.

SULFITE MANAGEMENT

Sulfite plays a major role in wine as a preservative—to protect against microbial spoilage—and as an antioxidant.

The chemistry of sulfite is beyond the scope of this book, and accurate sulfite management requires advanced laboratory experience. As a home winemaker though, you still need to manage sulfite additions to ensure that the wine is adequately protected without adding too little or too much, which could otherwise have a negative impact on the quality of the wine. Let's take a look at some very basic sulfite concepts to help you make informed decisions when adding sulfite.

Simplistically, the "active ingredient" in sulfite is sulfur dioxide (SO_2), which is the gas produced by burning elemental sulfur. Sulfur gas is easily recognized as an unpleasant and pungent burnt-match smell. Sulfur gas is great for storing empty oak barrels, for example, but it is not easily dissolved into solution for use in home winemaking. SO_2 can be sourced from sulfite, or its more specific names, potassium or sodium metabisulfite, by preparing an aqueous solution. When the solution is added to wine, SO_2 is released and begins doing its work. There are actually several forms of SO_2, but as a budding home winemaker, you only need be concerned with what is called *free SO_2*, which is the specific form of SO_2 that protects the wine; its concentration is measured in parts per million (ppm) or mg/L. In literature and conversations, *free SO_2* is often used interchangeably with *sulfite*. Although this is technically incorrect, it is always understood what is meant; but it's worth remembering that *sulfite* is what you add to wine and *free SO_2* is what protects it.

To complicate matters, free SO_2 combines or dissipates over time and becomes ineffective; therefore, more sulfite is required to protect the wine. So, how much sulfite to add? When? How do you measure free SO_2? What are the recommended levels of additions and concentrations?

Generally, it is recommended to add sulfite immediately upon the end of the alcoholic fermentation—in the stabilization phase—and before bottling. Some kits may combine both additions into one at stabilization and none at bottling; for example, they may provide sulfite to add 100 mg/L of free SO_2 instead of twice 50 mg/L. And if the wine is to be aged for an extended period of time, add more sulfite every 2–3 months; simply dissolve a pinch of powder, or the equivalent of the tip of a teaspoon, in a little water, add to the wine, and stir well.

Measuring free SO_2 requires advanced tools and techniques beyond the scope of this book and most home winemakers; however, if you follow the recommended addition timetable, you will not encounter any problems. Generally, you need 35–50 mg/L of free SO_2 from the end of fermentation to bottling, and assume a fairly low concentration (e.g., 5–10 mg/L) when ready to add sulfite. For example, if you assume that your wine contains 10 mg/L of free SO_2 and that your target is 35 mg/L, then you need to add 25 mg/L.

Table 6.2 provides the amount of sulfite required, as a powder, Campden tablets, or a 10% solution, to add 10, 35, or 50 mg/L of free SO_2 to a 23-L (6-gal) batch of wine. Use the lower end for red wine as these need less protection from sulfite, and use the higher end for whites, which are more delicate and more prone to oxidative and spoilage effects. In the example above where 25 mg/L of free SO_2 is to be added, this can be achieved by adding 2.5 × 0.4 g of powder, 2½ Campden tablets, or 2.5 × 4 mL of 10% solution.

Table 6.2. Sulfite additions

Sulfite form	Amount of free SO_2 to be added		
	10 mg/L	35 mg/L	50 mg/L
Powder	0.4 g	1.4 g	2.0 g
Campden tablets	1 tablet	3¼ tablets	4¾ tablets
10% solution	4 mL	14 mL	20 mL

If you have access to a pH meter and can measure pH, guide your sulfite additions based on the pH value. At higher pH, free SO_2 is less effective; therefore, more sulfite is required to provide the same level of protection. For anything above a pH of 3.5, increase the maximum rate of addition (i.e., 50 mg/L) by 10 mg/L for each 0.1 unit of pH over 3.5. For example, for a wine with a pH of 3.7, you would add 70 mg/L. A sulfite calculator is available at http://www.winemakermag.com/guide if you want to perform other calculations.

To add sulfite as a powder, weigh the required amount, dissolve thoroughly in cool water, add to the batch of wine, and stir thoroughly. Sulfite does not dissolve easily in water, so be sure to stir vigorously until all the powder has dissolved.

To add sulfite using Campden tablets, crush all tablets into a powder with a mortar and pestle, and follow the above instructions. Split a tablet in halves and quarters with a sharp knife if you need portions of a tablet. Campden tablets are very useful because you do not need to weigh them—as opposed to powder—and each weighs 0.44 g.

To add sulfite as a 10% solution, first prepare the solution by weighing 10 g (approximately 2 tsp) of sulfite powder and dissolving it in enough water to prepare 100 mL (3½ fl oz) of solution. Use a 10-mL syringe to draw the amount of solution required.

COLD STABILIZATION

Cold stabilization, or tartrate stabilization, is the process of ensuring that wine does not throw tartrate crystals when subjected to cold temperatures. If you have ever found colorless crystals—or, wine diamonds—in a bottle of white wine forgotten at the back of the fridge, then you know something about cold stabilization.

The crystals are the result of wine being stored at cold temperatures but not having been cold stabilized. In red wines, the crystals absorb some red pigments from the wine and are therefore reddish in color. Although completely harmless, these crystals affect the appearance of wine because they form at the bottom of the bottle or on the face of the cork exposed to wine.

This is not a problem in four- or five-week kit wines since manufacturers completely stabilize the juice to ensure tartrate-free wines; however, if you do come across a kit wine that precipitates tartrates, you have two options for your next batch.

The first and preferred option is to store your carboy of finished wine in a refrigerator set at the coldest temperature, ideally below 4°C (39°F), and to let stand for a minimum of two weeks. At the end of the cold stabilization period, you will see tartrate crystals at the bottom and sides of the carboy; then carefully rack the wine into another carboy. This is a natural process commonly used in commercial winemaking where the temperature is dropped to as low as –10°C (14°F) to hasten the process. As there could be a noticeable drop in acidity after cold stabilization, taste the wine and adjust acidity as needed by adding tartaric acid in small increments.

The second option is to add metatartaric acid. Dissolve ½ tsp of metatartaric acid powder in 25 mL of cold water and stir well. Add the metatartaric solution to wine just before filtration or bottling, and stir thoroughly. Be sure to store metatartaric acid powder in the refrigerator because it quickly loses effectiveness when stored at room temperature. For this reason, store wines treated with metatartaric acid in a cool cellar and drink them early, before the cellar temperature starts rising.

MALOLACTIC FERMENTATION

Malolactic fermentation (MLF) is the partial or complete transformation of naturally occurring, sharper tasting malic acid (think green apples) into the softer lactic acid (think milk) induced by indigenous or cultured lactic acid bacteria (LAB). MLF is almost exclusively used in red winemaking to lower and soften acidity; but often, it is also used in certain select whites, such as Chardonnay, to impart buttery aromas and mouthfeel, or to naturally reduce the acidity, rather than masking it with sugar.

Kits are designed and manufactured to ensure stability in the juice and the finished wine by annihilating bacteria (during pasteurization); therefore, they cannot be subjected to MLF and should *never* be attempted. MLF is strictly the domain of winemaking from fresh grape juice or grapes.

To learn more about MLF, refer to *Techniques in Home Winemaking* (Véhicule Press, 2008).

> WARNING: If you decide to experiment with MLF (by adding cultured LAB), do *not* add potassium sorbate, which will otherwise react with the bacteria and cause an off-smell of geraniums (more chemical than flowery).

BLENDING

Blending refers to the practice of mixing different batches of wine to achieve a desired style. Many great wines of the world, such as Bordeaux reds and California Meritage, are blends of two or more varietals from the same vintage, or blends of various batches, or *cuvées*, from different vintages as in the case of non-vintage champagne, for example. In Châteauneuf-du-Pape, a French winemaking area in southern France's Provence region, actually allows up to thirteen different varietals to be blended together. Blending is therefore considered sort of an art as it requires considerable skills, mastery and experience to be performed well.

Unless you seek to experiment with this art to blend different wines, this is generally not required with kits since these have been designed to produce an intended style. It will, however, come in very handy when a batch of wine has not turned out as expected or the wine has some minor fault that needs to be "corrected." It is often possible to eliminate—or at least, mask—a fault by blending wines; however, you should never blend a perfectly good wine with a seriously flawed wine in an attempt to correct or mask the problem; the result will be a mediocre wine, at best.

Blending can, however, be used effectively to improve balance in color, taste, aromas, flavors and mouthfeel in wines slightly out of balance. For example, blending is recommended for adjusting acidity and sweetness, alcohol level, mouthfeel (astringency), or for augmenting color in reds that are too light.

Before attempting to blend different wines, establish clear objectives—for example, are you trying to add depth to color, increase acidity, or reduce harshness? Next, determine which wines you will need to help you achieve your objectives. If you want to reduce alcohol level, you will need one or more batches with lower alcohol contents.

To zero in on a possible blend that achieves desired results, perform bench trials on as many combinations and permutations of the various batches, and vary the proportions of each. Have plenty of tasting glasses available. And always keep in mind the guiding principles presented in section *Managing total acidity (TA) and pH* to help narrow your work. The idea is to try as many blends as is practically possible; however, remember, you can blend to achieve the "numbers," but ultimately, you should let your taste guide you in the final decision and blend.

Blend all wines selected in creating the final wine in a large container capable of holding the total volume to ensure that each bottle of wine will be of consistent quality.

To determine total acidity (TA) or alcohol content of the final blend or of any component wines, use the Pearson Square:

where:
A = concentration of the wine to be used
B = concentration of the wine to be "corrected"
C = calculated or desired concentration
D = number of parts of wine to be used and is equal to $C - B$
E = number of parts of wine to be "corrected" and is equal to $A - C$

Example
A final alcohol level of 12.5% (*C*) is desired by blending two wines hav-

ing 13.5% (*A*) and 12% (*B*) alcohol, respectively. Plug these values into the Pearson Square as follows:

13.5		0.5
	12.5	
12		1

Therefore, $D = C - B = 12.5 - 12 = 0.5$, and $E = A - C = 13.5 - 12.5 = 1$. This means that for every part or volume (L or gal) of the 13.5% alc./vol. wine, you need to blend twice the amount of the 12% alc./vol. wine to achieve a wine with 12.5% alc./vol. A similar calculation can be done for total acidity.

Appendices

APPENDIX A—CONVERSION FACTORS BETWEEN METRIC, IMPERIAL AND US SYSTEMS

Table A.1. List of abbreviations for systems and units of measure used in this book.

Unit of measure	Abbreviation
alcohol per unit volume	alc./vol.
Brix degrees	°B
centimeter	cm
cup	cup
degrees Celsius	°C
degrees Fahrenheit	°F
fluid ounce	fl oz
foot (feet)	ft
gallon	gal
gram	g
Imperial	Imp
inch	in
kilogram	kg
liter	L
meter	m
milligram	mg
milliliter	cc *or* mL
millimeter	mm
ounce	oz
pound	lb
specific gravity	SG *or* sp gr
tablespoon	tbsp
teaspoon	tsp
United States	US
volume	vol
weight	wt

Length
1 cm = 10 mm = 0.39 in
1 in = 2.54 cm
1 m = 39.37 in = 3.28 ft = 1.09 yd
1 ft = 0.30 m

Mass and Weight
1 g = 0.035 oz
1 kg = 2.2 lb
1 lb = 16 oz = 454 g
1 oz = 28.35 g

Volume
1 L = 0.26 US gal = 0.22 Imp gal
23 L = 6 US gal = 5 Imp gal
1 US gal = 128 US fl oz = 0.83 Imp gal = 3.79 L
1 Imp gal = 160 Imp fl oz = 1.2 US gal = 4.55 L
1 mL = 0.034 US fl oz = 0.035 Imp fl oz
1 US fl oz = 29.57 mL
1 Imp fl oz = 28.41 mL
1 tsp = 5 mL
1 tbsp = 3 tsp = 15 mL
1 cup = 8 US fl oz = 237 mL

Concentration and Density
1 ppm = 1 mg/L (based on a density of 1 g per mL)
1000 ppm = 0.01 lb/gal (based on a density of 1¼ oz per US fl oz)

Temperature
$°F = 9/5 × (°C) + 32$
$°C = 5/9 × [(°F) – 32]$

NOTE: All equivalents are approximate because of rounding.

KIT INFORMATION

Name & Style: _____   Purchase Date: _____   Price: $ _____

JUICE PREPARATION

Day No. & Date	Additives/qty	SG	PA	Temp.	TA	pH	Notes
1.							
			(a)				

FERMENTATION

Day No. & Date	Additives/qty	SG	PA	Temp.	free SO$_2$	TA	pH	Notes
	END OF FERM.		(b)					

Final PA = (a−b) [   ] %alc./vol.

STABILIZATION & CLARIFICATION

Day No. & Date	Additives/qty			Temp.	free SO$_2$	TA	pH	Notes

Log Chart (continued)

FILTRATION

Day No. & Date	Additives/qty	Temp.	free SO$_2$	TA	pH	Notes

BOTTLING & AGING

Day No. & Date	Additives/qty	Temp.	free SO$_2$	TA	pH	Notes

TASTING NOTES

Glossary

aging: The practice of letting wine age, in bulk or in bottles, to allow it to develop its character, structure and to increase its complexity; also known as *maturation* or *cellaring*.

air lock: A device mounted on a bung that allows fermentation gas to escape from a carboy without letting air in; also known as a *fermentation lock*.

alcoholic fermentation: The chemical process of converting sugar in must into alcohol under the action of yeast with carbon dioxide (CO_2) gas as a by-product of this process.

amelioration: A method of reducing acidity by adding water to wine.

bench trials: Tests carried out on small volumes of wine to determine the effects of adding an ingredient, such as sugar or a fining agent, at various, pre-determined rates. Once the desired result is achieved, the ingredient is added at the determined rate of addition to the whole batch of wine.

bentonite: A natural absorptive type of clay that binds to and precipitates suspended particles.

blending: The practice of mixing different batches of wine to achieve a desired style, to improve balance in color, taste, aromas, flavors and mouthfeel, or to "correct" a wine fault.

blush: The American word for *rosé* wine.

bottle shock: A condition that may alter—if only for a short period of time—the character of a wine immediately following filtration and bottling operations as a result of extensive handling.

bottling: The final winemaking operation when wine is transferred from bulk containers to bottles for further aging or for drinking.

Brix (°B): An absolute measure of the density of sugar in juice or wine where 1°B represents 1 g of sugar in 100 g of solution, or 1% wt/wt.

bubbly: Another term for *sparkling wine*.

bung: A silicone or rubber stopper used on carboys, and equipped with a fermentation lock to allow fermentation gas to escape without letting air in.

Campden tablets: Sulfite-containing tablets for dissolving in water to prepare a sulfite solution for sanitizing equipment or for adding to wine as a stabilizing agent.

carbon dioxide (CO_2): A gas; a by-product of alcoholic fermentation.

carboy: A glass container used for making wine; usually 23 L (6 gal) in volume.

cellaring: The practice of letting wine age, in bulk or in bottles, to allow it to develop its character and structure, and to increase its complexity; also known as *aging* or *maturation*.

champagne: Sparkling wine produced strictly in the Champagne region of France using the traditional method—that is, a second alcoholic fermentation occurs in the bottle to trap the gas—but also commonly (though legally not correct) used for referring to any sparkling wine produced in this method.

chaptalization: The practice of adding fermentable sugar to juice to increase the potential alcohol level of wine, or adding sugar or other sweetening agents to a finished wine to increase sweetness.

Charmat: A method for making sparkling wines by carrying out a second alcoholic fermentation in bulk in tanks; also known as *cuve close* method.

chitosan: A shellfish-derived fining agent used in conjunction with kieselsol.

clarification: The process of removing particles still in suspension that affect clarity and limpidity in wine. Racking, fining and filtration are specific clarification processes.

CO_2: Chemical formula for *carbon dioxide*, a gas by-product of alcoholic fermentation.

cold stabilization: The process of ensuring that wine does not throw crystals, or *tartrates*, when subjected to cold temperatures; also known as *tartrate stabilization*.

concentrate: The term used for referring to concentrated juice or a blend of concentrated juice and grape juice.

conditioner: Liquid-invert sugar with, most often, a yeast inhibitor, such as potassium sorbate and sulfite, used for sweetening wine.

counterfining: The practice of adding a fining agent, such as bentonite, before fermentation, to help wine clarify in the later stages of winemaking.

cuve close: A method for making sparkling wines by carrying out a second alcoholic fermentation in bulk in tanks; also known as *Charmat* method.

cuvée: A batch of wine.

DAP: Abbreviation for *diammonium phosphate.*

diammonium phosphate (DAP): Yeast nutrients for boosting the
yeast's fermentation ability, thereby reducing the risk of a stuck or
sluggish fermentation.

disulfides: Foul-smelling compounds that cause wine to spoil.

dry: A wine style that has almost no residual sugar and no perceptible
sweetness; cf. *off-dry, medium-dry, medium-sweet* and *sweet.*

enzymes: Proteins that break down pectin, which occur naturally in wine
but are often the cause of cloudiness.

ethanol: The type of alcohol produced when sugar in grape juice is fermented.

fermentation: In winemaking, it refers to *yeast* or *alcoholic fermentation,*
the chemical process whereby yeast converts sugar in must into alcohol with carbon dioxide (CO_2) gas as a by-product; it can also
refer to *malolactic fermentation.*

fermentation lock: A device mounted on a bung that allows fermentation gas to escape from a carboy without letting air in; also known
as an *air lock.*

fermenter: Any container, such as a pail, carboy, or oak barrel, which is
used for fermenting juice into wine.

filtration: The process of passing wine through a filter medium by mechanical means to separate particles in suspension.

fining: The specific clarification process accomplished by adding a fining agent to wine.

free SO_2: The specific form of the sulfur dioxide (SO_2) compound that
provides protection against oxidation and microbial spoilage in wine.

fructose: A monosaccharide, or simple sugar, which can be fermented into alcohol. Sugar in grape juice is a source of fructose and glucose.

fruit wine: Usually refers to wine made from fruits other than grapes; for example, peach wine.

gelatin: A fining agent often used in conjunction with kieselsol.

glucose: A monosaccharide, or simple sugar, which can be fermented into alcohol. Sugar in grape juice is a source of fructose and glucose.

glycerin: An additive used for increasing mouthfeel and body, or perceived sweetness; also called *glycerol*.

glycerol: An additive used for increasing mouthfeel and body, or perceived sweetness; also called *glycerin*.

H$_2$S: Chemical formula for *hydrogen sulfide*, a foul-smelling compound responsible for imparting a rotten-egg smell to wine.

hydrogen sulfide (H$_2$S): A foul-smelling compound responsible for imparting a rotten-egg smell to wine resulting from, for example, excessive use of sulfur-based products, from nutrient deficiency during fermentation, and from extended contact with the lees during fermentation.

hydrometer: A simple instrument to measure the density, or *specific gravity (SG or sp gr)*, of sugar in juice and provides an approximate measure of *potential alcohol (PA)*. It is also used for monitoring fermentation progress by measuring the drop in density of wine.

ice wine: A very sweet wine produced from harvested grapes that have frozen naturally on vines.

inoculation: The process of adding, or *pitching*, yeast to juice to enable fermentation.

isinglass: A pure gelatin prepared from the swim bladders of cichlids (tropical spiny-finned freshwater fish) used as a fining agent.

J-tube: A rigid, inverted J-shaped tube used for racking wine; also known as a *racking cane*.

juice preparation: The process of reconstituting the concentrate by adding water, if required, to bring it to the required volume, and allowing the must (juice) to warm up or cool down to within the recommended range in preparation for fermentation.

kieselsol: A silicate suspension that electrostatically binds to and precipitates proteins.

KMS: Common abbreviation for potassium metabisulfite—a common sanitizing and stabilizing agent, and preservative.

lactic acid: A significant type of acid found in wine but not in grape juice. When present in wine, it is the result of malic acid having been converted by malolactic fermentation.

lactic acid bacteria (LAB): Bacteria that convert—by malolactic fermentation—the sharper malic acid in grape juice to the softer lactic acid in wine. Some other types of LAB can also cause spoilage.

lees: Dead yeast sediment resulting from yeast activity during alcoholic fermentation.

malic acid: A significant type of acid found in grape juice and wine; it is often converted into the softer lactic acid by malolactic fermentation.

malolactic fermentation (MLF): A secondary fermentation—typically not performed (not possible) in kit wines—where the sharper, naturally occurring malic acid is converted to the softer lactic acid under the action of lactic acid bacteria.

maturation: The practice of letting wine age, in bulk or in bottles, to allow it to develop its character and structure, and to increase its complexity; also known as *aging* or *cellaring*.

medium-dry: A wine style that lies between off-dry and medium-sweet in terms of perceptible sweetness; cf. *dry*, *off-dry*, *medium-sweet* and *sweet*.

medium-sweet: A wine style, not quite sweet, but with considerable perceptible sweetness; cf. *dry*, *off-dry*, *medium-dry* and *sweet*.

mercaptans: Foul-smelling compounds that cause wine to spoil.

metatartaric acid: An ingredient added to wine just before bottling to prevent tartrate crystals, which are the result of wine being subjected to cold temperatures.

***méthode traditionelle* (traditional method):** A method of making sparkling wines, such as champagne, by carrying out a second alcoholic fermentation in the bottle to trap the gas.

must: Unfermented juice.

oak: A type of wood used extensively, particularly in red winemaking, to add oak flavors and aromas, and complexity.

off-dry: A wine style, not quite dry, but with just a hint of perceptible sweetness; cf. *dry*, *medium-dry*, *medium-sweet* and *sweet*.

organoleptic: A descriptor used (as in "organoleptic qualities of the wine") for referring to the amalgam of color, taste, smell and mouthfeel.

oxidation: The chemical reaction between wine and air that causes premature aging or even spoilage if exposure to air becomes excessive.

pasteurization: A process for eradicating spoilage microorganisms, such as unwanted yeasts and bacteria, in juice destined for kits.

Pearson Square: An easy-to-use tool to calculate the number of parts of wine of a given concentration (i.e., alcohol content or TA) required to bring the concentration of another wine to a desired level.

pectin: A polysaccharide found in grape juice that can cause haze and cloudiness in wine.

pH: A measure of the strength of acids in a solution that provides an indication of the chemical stability of juice and wine. Water has a theoretical pH value of 7; anything less is acidic, anything higher is basic (alkaline).

pitching: The action of adding yeast to grape juice; see *inoculation*.

port: A fortified, sweet red wine made in the Oporto region in Portugal's Douro Valley.

potassium bicarbonate: An additive used for reducing acidity in wine.

potassium metabisulfite (KMS): A common sanitizing and stabilizing agent, and preservative.

potassium sorbate: A common food and beverage additive used for inhibiting growth of yeast and mold and prevent renewed fermentation in finished wines, most often in wines with residual sugar. It is often simply referred to as *sorbate* or *sorbic acid*.

potential alcohol (PA): The amount of alcohol that can be produced if all the fermentable sugar in the juice is allowed to ferment.

primary fermentation: The vigorous phase of alcoholic fermentation.

racking: The procedure for transferring wine from one container to another using a J-tube, or *racking cane*, to separate wine from sediment at the bottom of a container.

racking cane: A rigid, inverted-J-shaped tube used for racking wine.

residual sugar (RS): Unfermented sugar still remaining in a finished wine and which contributes sweetness.

rosé: A pink-colored wine made from red grape varieties using white winemaking techniques (although it can be a blend of white and red wines), and can range from dry to medium-sweet in style; also known as *blush*.

Saccharomyces bayanus: A popular species of winemaking yeasts used for difficult fermentation conditions.

Saccharomyces cerevisiae: The most common species of yeasts that is well suited for a wide range of winemaking applications.

sanitization: The process of washing and sanitizing all equipment to eliminate or inhibit microbes and avoid the risk of microbial contamination of juice or wine.

secondary fermentation: The less vigorous phase of alcoholic fermentation following the primary fermentation; also used for referring to *malolactic fermentation*.

second fermentation: In sparkling wine production, this refers to an additional alcoholic fermentation that occurs in bottles or in bulk in tanks. It is often used interchangeably with *secondary fermentation* though the meanings are different.

sherry: A fortified white wine made in Spain's Jerez region than can range from dry to sweet depending on style.

SO$_2$: Chemical formula for *sulfur dioxide*; often used interchangeably, though incorrect, with *sulfite*.

sodium metabisulfite: A common sanitizing agent also used, less commonly, as a stabilizing agent and preservative; see *potassium metabisulfite*.

sparkling wine: A style of wine with carbon dioxide (CO_2) produced by enabling a second alcoholic fermentation through the addition of sugar and yeast; also called *bubbly*.

specific gravity: A measure of the density of sugar in juice or wine relative to the density of water. It is commonly abbreviated to *SG* although *sp gr* is the correct form.

stabilization: The process of readying wine for consumption or aging to ensure that clarity, freshness and balance of the wine are maintained; and to protect the wine from microbial spoilage, refermentation and premature oxidation while the wine is aging and once in bottle. When used in a general sense, it can also include *cold stabilization*.

stuck or sluggish fermentation: A fermentation (alcoholic or malolactic) that has unexpectedly stopped completely or which is struggling and is slow to progress.

sulfite: A common stabilizing agent used in the food and beverage industry as an antioxidant and preservative; short for *potassium metabisulfite* or *sodium metabisulfite*.

sulfur dioxide (SO_2): The component of sulfite that provides protection although the term is often used interchangeably with *sulfite*.

sweet: A wine style with significant residual sugar (RS) content and, therefore, very sweet in taste; cf. *dry*, *off-dry*, *medium-dry* and *medium-sweet*.

tannin: A compound found or added to red wine to improve body, structure and mouthfeel by increasing astringency.

tartaric acid: The major and most important acid found in grape juice and wine.

tartrates: Deposits of harmless, colorless crystals—also known as *wine diamonds*—resulting from wine being subjected to cold temperatures.

tartrate stabilization: The process of ensuring that wine does not throw crystals, or *tartrates*, when subjected to cold temperatures; also known as *cold stabilization*.

topping: The practice of adding wine or water to bulk wine to reduce the headspace volume in carboys for minimizing exposure of wine to air.

total titratable acidity (TA): The concentration of titratable acids in juice and wine. The major contributing acids are tartaric, malic, lactic and citric acid; also called *total acidity* although not technically correct.

ullage: Headspace between the wine surface and the closure in a container.

varietal: Wine made from a single grape variety, for example, Chardonnay.

wine: An alcoholic beverage made by fermenting grape juice or other fruit juice. Wine from fruit juice is usually referred specifically to as *fruit wine*.

wine diamonds: Another term commonly used for referring to *tartrates*, the deposits of harmless, colorless crystals resulting from wine being subjected to cold temperatures.

winemaking: The process for producing wine, from juice preparation to bottling, by fermenting juice from grapes or other fruits.

wine thief: An elongated glass or plastic tube used for retrieving a small sample of wine from a container.

yeast: A fungus used for enabling fermentation of sugar into alcohol in winemaking.

yeast fermentation: Another term for *alcoholic fermentation*, the chemical process of converting sugar in must into alcohol under the action of yeast with carbon dioxide (CO_2) gas as a by-product; cf. *malolactic fermentation* where fermentation is enabled by bacteria.

yeast nutrients: Nutrients for boosting the yeast's fermentation ability, thereby reducing the risk of a stuck or sluggish fermentation.

Index

NOTE: Page numbers 91–101 in index entries refer to words defined in the Glossary.

bitterness, 77
blending, 18, 67–68, 81–83, 92
blush, 28, 92, 98.
    See also wine: rosé
body, 23, 25–26, 29
Bordeaux, 27, 30, 81
bottle shock, 64, 92
bottling, 18, 41, 61–64, 92
BPA. *See* bisphenol-A
brandy, 28
Brix, 22–23, 34, 92
bubbly, 92, 99.
    See wine: sparkling
bung, 92
Burgundy, 27–28

C

Cabernet Franc, 27–28, 30
Cabernet Sauvignon, 17, 27, 30
calcium carbonate, 77
Campden tablets, 18, 79–80, 92
carbon dioxide, 28, 34–35, 68,
    92–93
carboy, 39, 92
cellaring, 18, 91–92, 96.
    See also aging: wine
Chablis, 27–28
champagne, 29, 81, 92.
    See also wine: sparkling
Champagne, 92
chaptalization, 17, 75–76, 93
Chardonnay, 17, 25, 27–29, 81
Charmat, 29, 93.
    See also wine: sparkling
Châteauneuf-du-Pape, 81
chitosan, 25, 55, 93
clarification, 16, 18, 26, 41,
    52–57, 68, 93
clarifying agents, 18.
    See also fining: agents

cloudiness, 26, 68
CO_2, 93. *See* carbon dioxide
cold stabilization, 93.
    See stabilization: cold
color, 18, 23, 25, 60, 77, 82
concentrate, 14, 21–24, 29, 93
conditioner, 26, 93
copper sulfate, 70
corker, 37
corks, 37–39
counterfining, 43, 93
cream sherry, 28
cuve close, 29, 93.
    See also wine: sparkling
cuvée, 81, 94

D

DAP, 94.
    See diammonium phosphate
degassing, 53, 55–57, 68–69
diammonium phosphate, 24, 94
disulfides, 70, 94.
    See also hydrogen sulfide
dry, 94. *See* wine: dry.
    See also wine: styles

E

elderberries, 25–26
enzymes, 26, 30, 94
equipment
    bottling, 32–33
    starter fermentation, 31–32
ethanol, 94. *See* alcohol

F

fermentation, 16, 19, 25, 28,
    34–35, 41, 46–53,
    69, 78, 94
    alcoholic, 16, 48–52, 78, 91,
    94, 101

medium-dry, 94, 97.
> *See* wine: styles

medium-sweet, 94, 97.
> *See* wine: styles

mercaptans, 70, 97.
> *See also* hydrogen sulfide

Meritage, 81

Merlot, 27, 30

metatartaric acid, 97.
> *See* acid: metatartaric

méthode traditionelle, 29, 97.
> *See also* wine: sparkling

Mini Jet, 37–38

MLF, 96. *See* fermentation: malolactic

mold, 25. *See also* spoilage

mouthfeel, 18, 23, 25–27, 82

must, 16, 97

O

oak, 25–26, 28–29, 78, 97
> chips, 25–26

off-dry, 94, 97. *See* wine: styles

oloroso, 28

organoleptic qualities, 18, 29, 97

oxidation, 17, 49, 55, 58, 70, 79, 97

P

PA, 98. *See* potential alcohol

pasteurization, 22, 30, 81, 97

Pearson Square, 82–83, 97

pectic enzymes. *See* enzymes

pectin, 26, 98

PET, 39

pH, 76–77, 79, 98

Pinot Noir, 17, 27, 74

pitching, 95, 98. *See* inoculation

polyethylene tere-phthalate.
> *See* PET

port, 17, 27–28, 98
> styles, 28

potassium
> bicarbonate, 77, 98
> metabisulfite, 18, 25, 43, 53, 78, 98, 100
> sorbate, 18, 25–26, 53, 66, 68, 76, 81, 98

potential alcohol, 34–36, 46, 75, 95, 98

primary fermentation, 98.
> *See* fermentation: primary

R

racking, 17, 34–35, 50–51, 54, 68, 70, 98
> cane, 35, 96, 98

residual sugar, 98.
> *See* sugar: residual

Riesling, 27–28

rosé, 98. *See* wine: rosé

RS, 98. *See* sugar: residual

ruby port, 28

S

Saccharomyces bayanus, 16, 74–75, 99

Saccharomyces cerevisiae, 16, 74–75, 99

sanitization, 16, 41–43, 99

Sauvignon Blanc, 27

secondary fermentation, 99.
> *See* fermentation: secondary

second fermentation, 99.
> *See* fermentation: second

sediment, 17, 35–36, 51.
> *See also* lees

SG, 99. *See* specific gravity

sherry, 27–28, 99
> styles, 28

Notes